To Tina + Mike,
Happy Birthday
and Thank You
for FAMILY WORSHIP my
beautiful grand-
chidren.

Love
Mom
+ Gary Too

Family Worship

Edited by
Mark Kinzer
and
Jim Berlucchi

SERVANT BOOKS
Ann Arbor, Michigan

Originally published in 1988,
this edition was published in 1990 by
Servant Publications,
P.O. Box 8617,
Ann Arbor, MI 48107

Cover design by Michael Andaloro

90 91 92 93 94 10 9 8 7 6 5 4 3 2 1

Printed in the United States of America
ISBN 0-89283-695-4

Contents

Part I

Daily Family Prayer

ONE

Pattern for Daily Family Prayer

JUST AS AN INDIVIDUAL CHRISTIAN needs to come before the Lord daily in prayer, so a Christian family needs to come before the Lord daily with its praises, thanksgivings, and petitions. And just as an individual Christian needs to read and study Scripture, so a Christian family needs to build its common life on God's holy Word. Our daily prayer and study as individuals and as families honors God as the one who has created and redeemed us and fosters the life of God that is within us and among us.

Each family must discover the precise pattern that will work best for its own life together. Some families find that common prayer twice per day is practically feasible and spiritually advantageous. This pattern is in accord with the earliest Christian tradition of common prayer (corresponding, as in the Jewish tradition, with the two sacrifices offered daily in the temple—see Numbers 28:3-8). Other families find that they are only able to gather for prayer once per day. Each family must determine which pattern is most advisable for its life.

For most families the best time for a longer and more serious time of prayer and reading is in connection with the dinner hour. Some families find that the time before dinner works better for them, while others find that the time after dinner is optimal. Also, some families read the Bible together as part of their family prayer time. Other families read the Bible together and discuss it at another time (e.g., having family prayers before dinner, and reading the Bible together after dinner). It is important for every family to pray and study together regularly; the precise pattern may vary from family to family, and even within one family in different phases of its life.

The way each family approaches the reading and discussion of Scripture will certainly vary according to the number and age of its children. At one point, it might be best to simply read Bible stories from a children's Bible. At a later point, the children will be ready for a more adult reading and discussion.

Given this necessary diversity, are there some things that we can all do? The answer is, yes, by the grace of God! We can all seek to pray daily as families. We can all seek to read Scripture daily as families. Beyond these basics, we can also all seek to incorporate the Psalms into our prayer. The Book of Psalms is the Bible's own inspired prayer book, so when we pray the Psalms we know that we are praying according to the mind of God!

Praying the Psalms works best if you read them together as a family rather than having one person read and the others listen. Therefore, you need to decide on a common translation of the Psalms, and all the readers in your family need to have their own copy. Each psalm can be read together in its entirety, or you can read it antiphonally (dividing into two groups, and alternating by verse). Another method (that can also work with pre-readers) is to select a verse of the psalm as an antiphon and then repeat that verse corporately after every stanza of the psalm, while the psalm itself is read by one person.

Some of the psalms are quite long. Therefore, in the family

psalm sequence, the longest psalms are broken into two parts. However, some of the psalms and even half a psalm may still be too long for your family. If this is the case, it is fine to decide to only pray a certain section of the psalm. (This means that with longer psalms you will want to read the psalm in advance in order to pick a suitable breaking point.)

AN ORDER FOR DAILY PRAYER

The following is a recommended order of prayer. It can be varied according to time constraints and age of children, but the basic pattern is quite simple and can easily be adapted by most families. It goes as follows:

1. Call to Prayer

LEADER: O Lord, open my lips,
GROUP: *And my mouth shall declare your praise.*

2. Chorus or Song

3. Psalm

4. Scripture Reading
   (if the reading will be done in this context)

5. Chorus or Song
   This is especially appropriate if you will be taking the following period of extemporaneous prayer for charismatic worship (otherwise, you might want to exclude this second chorus/song)

6. Extemporaneous Prayer
   Petition, thanksgiving, or praise

7. The Lord's Prayer

POSTURE FOR PRAYER

It is best to stand for at least the first three sections of prayer (and perhaps for the entire prayer time, if there is no lengthy Scripture discussion). Standing is the main posture for prayer found in the Bible and expresses our attentiveness as servants of the King of kings.

WEDNESDAY PRAYER FOR GOD'S PEOPLE

On Wednesdays, it is recommended that you pray in particular for God's people. This fits best under section six above as a special petition. The responsive *Prayer for God's People*, which is included in chapter three of Part I, also fits best under section six of the daily prayer pattern.

SPECIAL SEASONAL PRAYERS

During the special seasons of the year, you may want to use additional prayers before dinner (such as the Advent prayers). These prayers should be treated as a separate prayer unit, and they should be prayed either before the above pattern begins (before the call to prayer) or after it ends (after the Lord's Prayer). The length of the special prayers may lead you to abbreviate some aspect of the daily pattern, which, of course, is a fine thing to do.

*   *   *   *   *

Let us joyfully come before our God as families and individuals and give him the glory and honor which is his due. To worship him is not a burden and a hardship, but is instead our greatest privilege as his sons and daughters. "For from him and through him and to him are all things. To him be glory for ever. Amen." **Rom 11:36**

TWO

Family Psalm Sequence

THE FOLLOWING SEQUENCE of psalms is built on a daily and weekly pattern. The daily pattern is expressed in the selection of psalms that are especially appropriate for the morning (e.g., Psalms 19, 100) and the evening (e.g., Psalms 134, 91, 4), though most of the psalms are appropriate at either time. The weekly pattern is expressed in the selection of Messianic psalms for Sunday, psalms of petition for Wednesday (and Friday morning, the day of the crucifixion), and Sabbath psalms for Friday night and Saturday (according to ancient Jewish tradition).

The following sequence of psalms is also built on a monthly pattern. The Sunday of Week One should always be the first Sunday of the month. For months with five Sundays, the psalms of Week Four should be repeated for the week of the fifth Sunday.

Finally, the psalm sequence is built on a yearly pattern. There are three monthly sequences (A, B, and C) to be used normally throughout the year (i.e., Ordinary Time): We will begin with sequence B (for 1990), and then use sequence C in 1991 and sequence A in 1992. We will return again to sequence B in 1993, and then continue the same rotation from year to year. During each of the special seasons of the year we follow a different sequence, and these patterns remain the same from year to year.

In addition to the psalm sequence, there is a sequence of brief New Testament readings that can be used as your family Scripture reading, or as a supplement to your Scripture reading (if your main time for study and discussion is outside the time of family prayers). If you want use another Scripture reading instead of the New Testament passage listed, feel free to do so. The listing of passages is intended as an option that can be used as it is found helpful.

Finally, a note on the numbering of the Psalms: there are two different ways to number the Psalms, though one (following the Hebrew text) is becoming predominant, and the other (following the ancient Greek translation of the Old Testament) is falling into disuse. We have followed the numbering used in the Revised Standard Version, New American Bible, New English Bible, New International Version, Jerusalem Bible, and most other translations. If, however, you are using the Gelineau version you will have to accommodate (in most cases, decrease the number given here by one).

Psalm Sequence for Ordinary Time
Year A

WEEK 1	SUN	MON	TUES	WED	THURS	FRI	SAT
Morning Psalm Reading	2 Acts 4:23-31	120 James 3:7-12	122 Eph. 2:19-22	9 2 Thes. 1:5-10	124 Col. 1:10-14	22 Mark 15:33-37	96 1 Thes. 4:16-18
Evening Psalm Reading	8 Heb. 2:5-9	121 Matt. 5:13-16	123 Matt. 5:17-19	10 Matt. 5:21-24	125 Matt. 5:27-30	29 Matt. 5:33-38	
WEEK 2							
Morning Psalm Reading	20 1 Jn. 5:1-5	126 Gal. 6:7-10	128 Eph. 3:14-19	11 Rom. 2:6-11	130 Eph. 2:4-7	35 John 15:18-21	97 Matt. 24:30-31
Evening Psalm Reading	21 Rev. 6:15-17	127 John 15:4-8	129 2 Cor. 4:7-12	12 James 3:3-6	131 Matt. 18:1-4	33 Rom. 8:22-25	
WEEK 3							
Morning Psalm Reading	16 Acts 2:22-28	132 Acts 2:29-33	138 Phil. 1:3-6	44 Rom. 8:35-39	139 John 1:47-50	41 John 13:16-20	98 Phil. 4:4-7
Evening Psalm Reading	24 Matt. 13:44-46	133 1 Thes. 4:9-12	134 1 Tim. 2:1-8	50 Heb. 13:14-16	141 Rev. 5:8-10	34 1 Pet. 3:8-12	
WEEK 4							
Morning Psalm Reading	45 Heb. 1:1-2	143 Rom. 12:12	3 2 Cor. 3:17-18	51 Heb. 9:13-14	5 Rom. 7:15-17	52 Col. 1:11-12	99 1 Pet. 1:13-16
Evening Psalm Reading	47 1 Tim. 5:13-16	144 1 Pet. 2:9-10	4 Eph. 4:25-28	60 Eph. 6:10-12	13 Eph. 6:13-17	92 Eph. 6:18-20	

Psalm Sequence for Ordinary Time
Year B

WEEK 1	SUN	MON	TUES	WED	THURS	FRI	SAT
Morning Psalm Reading	72 1 Cor. 15:16-19	14 Eph. 5:15-17	19 Rom. 11:33-36	68 Rev. 12:10-11	25 Matt. 11:28-30	54 2 Tim. 4:17-18	135 Matt. 16:24-26
Evening Psalm Reading	110 2 Cor. 9:6-8	15 2 Cor. 7:1	23 Heb. 13:20-21	74 1 Pet. 4:17-19	27 Matt. 6:19-21	93 1 Cor. 3:16-17	
WEEK 2							
Morning Psalm Reading	116 Col. 2:6-7	30 1 Jn. 1:5-7	32 Col. 3:8-10	75 2 Tim. 2:3-7	37a 2 Cor. 1:3-4	55 Luke 11:27-28	136 Gal. 2:20
Evening Psalm Reading	118 1 Pet. 2:7-8	31 Rom. 15:13	36 1 Tim. 1:15-17	77 James 1:2-4	37b Col. 3:16-17	95 Heb. 3:12-15	
WEEK 3							
Morning Psalm Reading	8 1 Cor. 15:51-52	43 Phil. 1:27	48 Gal. 5:13-14	78a Col. 3:12-13	57 Phil. 1:9-11	69 John 2:15-17	29 Phil. 3:20-21
Evening Psalm Reading	2 Luke 11:9-10	46 1 Jn. 2:1-2	49 1 Tim. 6:6-8	78b James 1:5-6	56 Heb. 13:5-6	96 2 Tim. 2:11-12	
WEEK 4							
Morning Psalm Reading	21 Rom. 6:5-6	59 2 Tim. 2:20-21	62 2 Thes. 1:11-12	79 1 Jn. 2:3-6	64 1 Tim. 2:8-10	86 Gal. 5:24-26	33 2 Cor. 4:16-18
Evening Psalm Reading	20 2 Pet. 3:11-13	61 James 1:9-10	63 Col. 3:14-15	80 Phil. 1:20-21	65 2 Cor. 1:21-22	97 1 Jn. 2:9-11	

Psalm Divisions: 37a: 1-24;   78a: 1-39;
37b: 25-40;   78b: 40-72

Psalm Sequence for Ordinary Time
Year C

WEEK 1	SUN	MON	TUES	WED	THURS	FRI	SAT
Morning Psalm Reading	24 1 Cor. 15:20-22	66 Rev. 3:19-20	70 1 Jn. 2:15-17	83 Phil. 4:8	81 2 Tim. 2:22-23	88 1 Tim. 3:16	34 1 Cor. 12:4-7
Evening Psalm Reading	16 1 Jn. 4:19-21	67 Phil. 2:1-2	71 James 1:12	85 Titus 3:1-2	84 Col. 3:18-19	98 2 Pet. 1:5-7	
WEEK 2							
Morning Psalm Reading	47 Luke 24:45-47	89a 1 Tim. 6:9-10	100 Phil. 2:3-4	94 James 5:19-20	101 2 Thes. 3:3-5	102 1 Cor. 9:12-13	92 Gal. 6:1-2
Evening Psalm Reading	45 1 Jn. 4:10-12	89b Col. 3:20-21	91 Jude 20-23	137 2 Tim. 3:14-15	103 James 1:19-21	99 1 Jn. 3:4-6	
WEEK 3							
Morning Psalm Reading	110 Eph. 1:22-23	104a 2 Tim. 3:16-17	111 1 Cor. 13:4-6	105a Titus 2:11-14	113 2 Pet. 1:3-4	140 1 Jn. 4:7-9	93 2 Thes. 2:16-17
Evening Psalm Reading	72 Acts 2:43-45	104b 1 Cor. 2:14-16	112 Col. 3:23-24	105b 1 Jn. 3:7-8	114 Phil. 2:12-13	135 James 1:22-25	
WEEK 4							
Morning Psalm Reading	118 1 Cor. 15:3-5	145 1 Tim. 6:11-12	147 James 1:26-27	106a 2 Tim. 4:6-8	149 1 Jn. 3:23-24	142 Phil. 3:12-14	95 1 Cor. 6:19-20
Evening Psalm Reading	116 Phil. 4:12-13	146 1 Jn. 3:16-18	148 2 Cor. 12:9-10	106b Gal. 6:14-15	150 Col. 4:5-6	136 James 5:13-14	

Psalms Divisions: 89a: 1-18; 104a: 1-23; 105a: 1-22; 106a: 1-23;
89b: 19-51; 104b: 24-35; 105b: 23-45 106b: 24-48

Psalm Sequences for Special Seasons

Advent

FIRST 2 WEEKS	SUN	MON	TUES	WED	THURS	FRI	SAT
Morning Psalm Reading	93 Matt. 24:36-39	94 Mark 13:33-35	9 Mark 1:4-5	7 Mark 1:6-8	62 2 Pet. 3:8-10	28 2 Pet. 3:11-13	97 1 Thes. 5:16-24
Evening Psalm Reading	95 1 Thes. 4:13-15	50 1 Thes. 4:16-18	10 1 Thes. 5:1-3	17 1 Thes. 5:4-7	75 1 Thes. 5:8-11	96 2 Pet. 3:14-15	
SECOND 2 WEEKS							
Morning Psalm Reading	98 Rom. 13:11-12	46 Luke 1:26-29	76 Luke 1:30-33	87 1 Cor. 1:6-8	132 1 Cor. 4:5	96 1 Thes. 3:12-13	98 1 Thes. 5:16-24
Evening Psalm Reading	99 Rom. 13:13-14	48 Phil. 4:4-7	84 2 Thes. 1:6-8	122 Phil. 3:18-21	147 James 5:7-9	97 James 5:10-11	

Christmas

TWELVE DAYS	SUN	MON	TUES	WED	THURS	FRI	SAT
Morning Psalm Reading	2 Heb. 1:1-3	146 Gal. 4:4-5	147 Gal. 4:6-7	148 Eph. 2:4-5	149 Col. 1:13-16	150 Col. 1:19-20	132 Eph. 3:1
Evening Psalm Reading	21 Jn. 1:9-13	8 1 Jn. 1:1-3	45 Tit. 3:4-5	72 Tit. 3:6-7	85 Col. 1:17-18	110 Eph. 3:8-10	

Psalm Sequences for Special Seasons
Forty Days*

FIRST 2 WEEKS	SUN	MON	TUES	WED	THURS	FRI	SAT
Morning Psalm Reading	15 Rev. 3:19-20	6 1 Cor. 9:24-27	38 Joel 2:12-13	51 Phil. 2:14-15	90 2 Pet. 3:8-9	143 Luke 5:30-32	28 1 Pet. 1:14-15
Evening Psalm Reading	25 2 Cor. 6:1-4a	32 Ex. 19:4-6	39 Rom. 12:1-2	88 Eph. 4:30-32	130 Heb. 13:12-15	40 2 Cor. 7:9-10	
MID 2 WEEKS							
Morning Psalm Reading	1 Luke 11:9-10	119a 1 Cor. 1:18-19	119b 1 Cor. 1:27-30	119c 1 Tim. 2:4-6	119d Heb. 4:14-15	119e Heb. 9:11-12	119f 1 Jn. 2:8-10
Evening Psalm Reading	36 1 Pet. 5:10-11	73 Luke 12:29-31	42 Heb. 10:19-22	63 Heb. 12:12-13	84 Heb. 7:26-27	27 1 Jn. 1:8-9	
FINAL 2 WEEKS							
Morning Psalm Reading	2 2 Cor. 4:10-12	35 Rom. 5:8-10	52 Heb. 2:9-10	69 Rom. 5:6-8	22 Heb. 13:12-15	22 1 Pet. 2:21-24	23 1 Pet. 1:18-21
Evening Psalm Reading	18 1 Pet. 4:13-14	41 1 Cor. 1:22-24	102 Gal. 6:14	69 Jn. 12:24-26	55 Phil. 2:5-8	23 Jn. 10:11-16	

Psalm Divisions: 119a: 1-24; 119c: 57-88; 119e: 121-152;
119b: 25-56; 119d: 89-120; 119f: 153-176

*Note: This season is commonly called Lent in most liturgical traditions; however, we call the season the Forty Days in this book. This name emphasizes the scriptural origin of this time of repentance and fasting, referring in particular to the Israelites' forty years of wandering in the desert and Jesus' own forty-day fast before he began his public ministry.

Psalm Sequences for Special Seasons
Easter—Pentecost

FIRST 2 WEEKS	SUN	MON	TUES	WED	THURS	FRI	SAT
Morning Psalm Reading	45 Eph. 2:4-6	2 Col. 3:1-4	20 Acts 2:22-24	18 Acts 2:32-36	110 Acts 5:30-32	24 1 Pet. 3:18-19	47 Acts 10:40-43
Evening Psalm Reading	8 Heb. 10:12-14	16 Rom. 6:4	21 1 Pet. 1:3-5	72 1 Pet. 1:18-21	118 1 Pet. 2:4-5	132 1 Pet. 2:24-25	
MID 3 WEEKS							
Morning Psalm Reading	111 Luke 20:34-36	112 Jn. 5:28-29	115 Acts 24:14-15	117 Jn. 11:25-27	135 Rom. 8:10-11	107 Col. 1:12-14	96 1 Cor. 15:20-22
Evening Psalm Reading	112 Jn. 6:47	114 Acts 4:11-12	116 Jn. 6:38-40	118 Rom. 6:8-11	136 2 Cor. 5:14-15	98 Heb. 7:24-27	
FINAL 2 WEEKS							
Morning Psalm Reading	145 1 Cor. 12:13	146 Jn. 10:10	147 1 Pet. 2:9-10	148 1 Cor. 6:19-20	149 Gal. 5:22-23	150 Rom. 8:26-27	46 Gal. 5:16-18
Evening Psalm Reading	87 1 Pet. 3:21-22	47 Titus 3:5-7	24 Rom. 14:7-9	68 Rom. 8:14-17	132 Rom. 10:8-10	67 Acts 13:30-33	

THREE

Prayer for God's People

This prayer can be used on Wednesdays as a way of interceding for God's people (except it is inappropriate during the fifty days between Easter and Pentecost because of its penitential nature). The prayer has four topics: the restoration of Christian truth, holiness of life, unity, and witness. One could also use these four topics as a way of structuring a more extemporaneous time of prayer.

In this prayer we identify with the sin and infidelity of God's people, even as Daniel (Dan 9:5-11, 20) and Nehemiah (Neh 1:4-7) identified themselves with the transgressions of Israel. God relates to his people as a body. We stand before him in prayer not only as individuals, but also as representatives of his church. We may not have sinned personally in the ways mentioned in this prayer, but we have suffered personally from the effects of these sins, and we will all benefit greatly as God wipes them away.

LEADER: Let us pray now on behalf of the whole people of God.

Heavenly Father, God of steadfast love and faithfulness, we confess our sin before you.

You have called us to be the pillar and bulwark of the truth, but we have forsaken your Word and exchanged the truth for a lie.

GROUP: *Have mercy, Lord, and forgive our sin.*

LEADER: You have called us to be holy even as you are holy, but we have disobeyed your commandments and defiled your temple.

GROUP: *Have mercy, Lord, and forgive our sin.*

LEADER: You have called us to love one another and to maintain the unity of the Spirit in the bond of peace, but we have broken your Son's body with our enmity and strife.

GROUP: *Have mercy, Lord, and forgive our sin.*

LEADER: You have called us to be the salt of the earth and the light of the world, but we have imitated the nations, losing our flavor and hiding our light.

GROUP: *Have mercy, Lord, and forgive our sin.*

LEADER: Have mercy, Lord our God, on the people called by your name. Rule us by your Word, sanctify us by your Spirit, unite us in your love, and work through us by your power. May the glory of Christ so shine upon us that the nations may come and behold his beauty, and may the knowledge of you fill the earth as the waters cover the sea.

GROUP: *For yours is the kingdom, the power, and the glory forever and ever. Amen.*

Part II

The Lord's Day Celebration

ONE

An Introduction to Celebrating the Lord's Day

IN THE BOOK OF Nehemiah, there is a passage which is puzzling to many people today:

> And Nehemiah, who was the governor, and Ezra the priest and scribe, and the Levites who taught the people said to all the people, "This day is holy to the Lord your God; do not mourn or weep." For all the people wept when they heard the words of the law. Then he said to them, "Go your way, eat the fat and drink sweet wine and send portions to him for whom nothing is prepared; for this day is holy to our Lord; and do not be grieved, for the joy of the Lord is your strength." **Neh 8:9-10**

It is puzzling because we have lost an understanding of celebration (and of mourning as well). The people described in the passage had just heard and understood the words of the law, and they had discovered that they were not keeping them. They began to mourn out of repentance when Nehemiah, Ezra, and the Levites told the people not to mourn. They said that the people should rejoice because the

25

day was holy to the Lord (the first day of the seventh month, "the feast of trumpets," cf. Lv 23:23-25; Nm 29:1-6). So the people began to celebrate.

This passage illustrates some important truths for us. It shows, first of all, that joy or rejoicing is more than feeling happy. When the Levites told the people to rejoice, they told them to hold a feast. They told them, in other words, to celebrate. Rejoicing (or joy) for the Israelites was not just a feeling, but it was something they did. To rejoice is to celebrate, to express the goodness of the occasion in a joyful way. We can see this also in the Book of Deuteronomy when it instructs the people to celebrate the great feasts like Passover, Weeks, and Tabernacles. It tells them to come to Jerusalem, make an offering, and "rejoice before the Lord your God" (16:11), that is, it tells them to celebrate in God's presence.

We celebrate certain days or events because it is good and right to do so. It would not have been proper for the Israelites to mourn on a festival day. We celebrate because celebrating is a way of honoring God. Nehemiah, Ezra, and the Levites told the people that the day was "holy to the Lord your God." That meant that it was set apart (holy) to honor the Lord. The people, therefore, were supposed to celebrate in order to honor the Lord. Finally, we celebrate as an expression of gratitude for the good things God has done for us.

Celebrating is also a great benefit to us. "The joy of the Lord (rejoicing in the Lord) is our strength." When we celebrate God's goodness and what he has done for us, we are strengthened and refreshed. Our God is a God who wishes us to share his joy (and his strength) when we worship him. To be sure, sometimes we should worship him soberly, humbling ourselves in repentance and mourning. But the main times of worship under the old covenant and the new covenant are times of celebration—rejoicing in God's presence. The Lord's Day is one of these times of celebration.

THE EARLY CHRISTIANS CELEBRATED
THE LORD'S DAY

We can see in the Scripture indications that the early Christians observed the Lord's Day. John, in the Book of Revelation, says, "I was in the Spirit on the Lord's Day" (1:10). Likewise, we read of Paul gathering with the Christians at Troas on the first day of the week (Acts 20:7) and instructing the Christians at Corinth to set aside contributions for the community at Jerusalem on the first day of the week (1 Cor 16:2). Sunday seems to have been a special day for the first Christians and was used as a day for gathering together. Probably it was the day of assembly because it commemorated the resurrection of the Lord which had occurred on Sunday.

The earliest writings from within a hundred years of the death of the last apostle indicate even more clearly the way the Christians marked Sunday. Some of these writings explain what they understood the Lord's Day to be:

The celebration of the resurrection: Ignatius of Antioch, writing within twenty years of the death of the apostle John, said, "Let every friend of Christ keep the Lord's Day as a festival, the resurrection day, the queen and chief of all days of the week and on which our life sprang up again and victory over death was obtained in Christ."

To the Magnesians, 9

The celebration of creation and the new creation: Justin Martyr, a convert who was born and raised near Jacob's well, writing about forty years later, said, "But Sunday is the day on which we hold our common assembly, because it is the first day on which God, having wrought a change in the darkness and matter, made the world; and Jesus Christ, our Saviour, on the same day rose from the dead."

First Apology, 67

The celebration of the beginning of the age to come: The Epistle of Barnabas, written about the time Ignatius wrote, says, "I will make a beginning of the eighth day, that is, the beginning of another world. Wherefore, also we keep the eighth day with joyfulness, the day on which Jesus rose again from the dead." section 15

Since Sunday was the day after the seventh day, it was the eighth day as well as the first day. Since the seven days symbolized God's original creation of the world, the eighth day can be seen as the beginning of the new creation, the world to come. In the New Testament as well (1 Pt 3:20; 2 Pt 2:5) the number eight seems to have been seen as a symbol of the new creation. The early Christians knew that they were participating through the Spirit in the age to come and prayed on the Lord's Day that Jesus might come and bring in the new age completely: "Come, Lord Jesus!" (Rv 22:20).

SUNDAY IS THE LORD'S DAY FOR CHRISTIANS

Sunday, then, is the weekly celebration of the Christian people. It is the day on which they gather together to celebrate the resurrection, the completion of the work of redemption, the day in which the new creation was inaugurated and therefore the day on which the age to come was opened to the human race. It is the day on which the true sun of righteousness rose with healing in his rays (Mal 4:2). Just as Easter is the major yearly celebration for Christians, so Sunday is the major weekly celebration for Christians. It is a day to rejoice in our hope (Rom 12:12).

The celebration of the Lord's Day holds a similar place for Christians to the place the celebration of the Sabbath held for Jews. Christians who were not born or circumcised as Jews were not obligated by the New Testament to keep the seventh day (cf. Col 2:16; Gal 4:10). That was the day of celebration for those who were under the Mosaic law. However, Christians since then have usually seen a connection between the Sabbath and the Lord's Day.

Some Christians have said simply that the Lord's Day is the Christian Sabbath. Christians keep the Sabbath commandment on Sunday rather than Saturday, and so Sunday is the new covenant Sabbath. Others have said that the Sabbath commandment was given to teach that one day a week should be set aside for the worship of God. Christians have to keep the commandment, but they do not have to do it on the seventh day. Taking a day of rest and worship is part of God's purpose for the human race and therefore obligatory, but doing it on the seventh day was only obligatory for the Jews. For Christians, it is more fitting to do so on the first day, the day of the resurrection. Finally, other Christians have said that setting aside a day of rest and worship is not obligatory at all, but nonetheless it is very valuable to do, and one of the purposes of the Sabbath commandment is to teach us the value of such a custom. Although these views show some difference among Christians as to the relationship of the observance of the Lord's Day to the Sabbath commandment, almost all Christians see the importance of having such a day and accept the first day of the week, the Lord's Day, as the weekly day of celebration for Christians.

WHAT CHRISTIANS HAVE LEARNED ABOUT THE LORD'S DAY

There are many truths that Christians have learned from the Sabbath celebration and applied through the centuries. They have, as we have said, learned first of all the value of setting aside one day of the week for the worship of God. Such a custom is a way of honoring God as well as a means of spiritual growth. They have also learned the value of the day of rest. The true rest is to cease from our sins, but that rest is symbolized by a day of rest in which we cease from our work. Rest is not inactivity, but it is a change of activity. In this case, rest is ceasing from the work by which we support ourselves and maintain our life and instead taking on the activity of worshiping. It is therefore a day of gathering together, of prayer and Christian study, of giving alms and doing good (like visiting the sick). It is a day for the Christian community and for the family. It is not so much a "day off," though it can be that, but a day in which we do "not go our own ways or seek our own pleasure or talk idly" (Is 58:13), a day to honor God.

Finally, Christians have learned from the Sabbath that the Lord's Day is a time of celebration, a time to "take delight in the Lord." It is a day in which the joy of the Lord, rejoicing in the Lord, can be our strength. Here, especially, modern Christians need to learn something. They need to learn how to celebrate again. There was a time when Christians knew how to take a feast day and celebrate, and Christians in many places of the world still do. But for most Christians modern life has eroded an understanding of how to keep a feast. For that reason, we can learn again an old truth from the celebration of the Sabbath.

This part contains a way of making the Lord's Day a family or household celebration. The celebration here does not replace the communal worship service on Sunday any more than the Sabbath meal replaced the synagogue or temple services. Most especially, it is not a celebration of the Lord's Supper or Eucharist. Rather, it is a way of making the whole day a feast day. This part contains an order for an opening meal to begin the Lord's Day and a closing meal to conclude it. It is modeled on the Sabbath meals as Jesus and his disciples would probably have celebrated them, but the prayers have been changed to bring out the significance of the Lord's Day. It contains one way of making the Lord's Day a delight and a source of life for the whole Christian people. Those who have made use of it as a means of setting aside a day to celebrate the resurrection of the Lord have discovered that a day specially set apart for the Lord is a day which he blesses with his presence.

TWO

The Lord's Day Celebration

"Leader" is the head of the household, most commonly the father of the family. "Assistant" is either the person next in authority or next in age to the Leader, most commonly the mother of the family. "Group" is all the household members and any guests who may be present. When the letters "G," "A," and "L" appear in parentheses, it indicates that the reading may be done responsively as marked, if more group participation is desired for some special reason, like the desire to adapt the celebration to the presence of small children.

THE LIGHTING OF THE CANDLE

The Assistant usually presides over the Lighting of the Candle. For a shortened form of the ceremony you may omit the passage from John 1:1-5.

ASSISTANT: In the beginning was the Word and the Word was with God and the Word was God.

(G:) *All things were made through him and without him nothing was made that has been made.*

(A:) In him was life and the life was the light of men.

(G:) *The light shines in the darkness and the darkness has not overcome it (Jn 1:1-5).*

ASSISTANT: Heavenly Father, in honor of your Son, Light of the world and Author of life, we are about to kindle the light for the Lord's Day. On this day you raised your Son Jesus from the dead and began the new creation. May our celebration of his resurrection this day be filled with your peace and heavenly blessing. Be gracious to us and cause your Holy Spirit to dwell more richly among us.

Father of mercy, continue your loving kindness toward us. Make us worthy to walk in the way of your Son, loyal to your teaching and unwavering in love and service. Keep far from us all anxiety, darkness, and gloom; and grant that peace, light, and joy ever abide among us.

GROUP: *For in you is the fountain of life; in your light do we see light.*

Light the candle and recite the following blessing:

ASSISTANT: Blessed are you, Lord our God, who created light on the first day and raised your Son, the Light of the world, to begin the new creation.

Blessed are you, Lord our God, King of the universe, who give us joy as we kindle the light for the Lord's Day.

GROUP: *Amen.*

For a short form of the ceremony, the following set of exhortations and responses may be omitted.

LEADER: Let us trust in the Lord and his saving help.

GROUP: *The Lord is my light and my salvation.*

LEADER: Let us receive his life and rejoice in his presence.

GROUP: *He is the true Light that enlightens every man.*

LEADER: Let us keep his commandments and walk in his ways.

GROUP: *His Word is a lamp to my feet and a light for my path.*

LEADER: Let us proclaim his goodness and show forth his glory.

GROUP: *We are the light of the world and the salt of the earth.*

THE BLESSING OF THE MEAL
AND THE SETTING-ASIDE OF THE DAY

The Opening Proclamation

The following blessing is a proclamation to introduce the meal and normally would be said entirely by the Leader but can also be read responsively, as indicated.

LEADER: Brothers and sisters, this is the Lord's Day.

(G:)   *Let us welcome it in joy and peace.*

(L:)   Today we set aside the concerns of the week that we may honor the Lord and celebrate his resurrection. Today we cease from our work in order to worship God and remember the eternal life to which he has called us.

(G:)   *The Lord himself is with us, to refresh and strengthen us.*

(L:)   Let us welcome God among us and give him glory.

(G:)   *Let us love one another in Christ.*

(L:)   May the Holy Spirit be with us, to deepen our devotion to the Lord and to increase our zeal for the way of life he has given us.

It is possible to insert here a song and/or a time of praise.

The Blessing of the Wine

Pour wine into the cup, raise it, and recite the following prayer.

LEADER: Let us praise God with this symbol of joy and thank him for the blessings of the past week— for health, strength, and wisdom, for our life together in (name of church/community to which the family belongs), for the discipline of our trials and temptations, for the happiness that has come to us out of our work.

The following section of the prayer will vary depending on the season. The Leader should pick the appropriate form.

Standard Form

LEADER: Let us thank him this day especially for the great blessings he has bestowed on us in Christ. From his fullness we have all received grace upon grace. We who were dead through sin have been brought to life together with Christ and raised up with him and made to sit in heavenly places with him. Lord our God, you have brought us into the rest of Christ.

GROUP: *Now we live with him through the Holy Spirit, and we look for the day when we will dwell with him in your everlasting kingdom.*

Advent

LEADER: Let us thank him this day especially for the salvation we receive in Christ. By his coming in the flesh he ransomed us from sin and the power of death, and by his coming again he will renew all things, destroy every evil, and establish the eternal reign of God on earth. Lord

our God, you have made us your sons and
daughters through Jesus Christ.

GROUP: *Now we live with him through the Holy Spirit, and we
look for the day when we will dwell with him in your
everlasting kingdom.*

Christmas Season—between Christmas and Epiphany

LEADER: Let us thank him this day especially for the
great blessings he has bestowed on us in Christ.
In him the fullness of God was pleased to dwell,
reconciling earth to heaven, and imparting to us
the fullness of life. In him the Word became
flesh, enabling men and women of flesh to
become children of God. Lord our God, you
have revealed to us your glory in Jesus your
Son and have made us partakers of the divine
nature.

GROUP: *Now we live with him through the Holy Spirit, and we
look for the day when we will dwell with him in your
everlasting kingdom.*

Forty Days

LEADER: Let us thank him this day especially for the
victory over sin that he won for us upon the
cross and for this season in which we turn our
eyes to him with renewed fervor, hungering
and thirsting for righteousness. Lord our God,
we have fasted this week that we might seek
your face.

GROUP: *And now we eat and drink with joy as we celebrate
your salvation.*

Easter Season—between Easter and Pentecost

LEADER: Let us thank him this day especially for the great victory he has won for us in Christ. By his resurrection he has triumphed over sin, conquered death, defeated Satan, and won for us the riches of an eternal inheritance. We who were perishing through sin have been brought to life together with Christ and raised up with him and made to sit in heavenly places with him. Lord our God, you have given us a new birth through the resurrection of Christ.

GROUP: *Now we live with him through the Holy Spirit, and we look for the day when we will dwell with him in your everlasting kingdom.*

From this point onward the prayer continues without seasonal variations.

LEADER: Blessed are you, Lord our God, King of the universe, who have created the fruit of the vine.

GROUP: *Amen.*

The Setting-Aside of the Day
This blessing welcomes the day and consecrates it to the celebration of the Lord's resurrection.

LEADER: Blessed are you, Lord our God, for the true rest you have given us in your Son Jesus and for this day which is a commemoration of his redeeming work. We welcome this day with gladness and consecrate it to the celebration of his resurrection and of the new creation founded in him. Look graciously upon your servants and show us your glory. Blessed are you, Lord our God, who favor your people in the days set aside to your honor.

GROUP: *Amen.*

The Leader drinks from the cup and passes it to the others present.

The Blessing of the Bread
The Leader takes bread and recites the following blessing.

LEADER: The eyes of all look to you, O Lord, and you give them their food in due season.

GROUP: *You open your hand, you satisfy the desire of every living thing.*

LEADER: Blessed are you, Lord our God, King of the universe, who bring forth bread from the earth.

GROUP: *Amen.*

Distribute the bread and begin the meal.

BLESSINGS AFTER THE MEAL

After the meal another cup of wine is poured, and the following blessings are recited with the cup raised.

LEADER: Let us bless the Lord.

GROUP: *Blessed be the name of the Lord from this time forth and forever.*

LEADER: Let us bless our God, of whose bounty we have partaken.

GROUP: *Blessed be our God, of whose bounty we have partaken and through whose goodness we live.*

LEADER: Blessed are you, Lord our God, who feed the whole world with your goodness, with grace, with steadfast love and mercy. Through your great goodness food has never failed us. May it not fail us for ever and ever, for your great name's sake, since you nourish and sustain all beings, and do good to all, and provide food for all your creatures whom you have created. Blessed are you, Lord our God, King of the universe, who give food to all.

GROUP: *Blessed be his name forever.*

LEADER: Blessed are you, Lord our God, for by your great mercy we have been born anew to a living hope through the resurrection of Jesus Christ from the dead and to an inheritance that is imperishable, undefiled, and unfading. Blessed are you, Lord our God, King of the universe, for giving us new life in your Son.

GROUP: *Blessed be his name forever.*

LEADER: Have mercy, Lord our God, upon your people who belong to your Son, the dwelling place of your Spirit. Grant that the Christian people throughout the world may attain the unity for which Jesus prayed on the eve of his sacrifice, and that we in (name of church/community to which the family belongs) may be a sign of that unity and a means of its growth. May all your people be renewed in the power of your Spirit so that we might be without spot or blemish and ready for your Son's return. Blessed are you, Lord our God, King of the universe, ruler and builder of your people.

GROUP: *Blessed be his name forever.*

As the cup is being passed, the Leader recites the following blessing from Numbers 6:24-26.

LEADER: May the Lord bless you and keep you; may the Lord make his face to shine upon you and be gracious to you; may the Lord lift up his countenance upon you and give you peace.

GROUP: *Amen.*

THREE

Closing Ceremony for Sunday Evening

BLESSING BEFORE THE MEAL

This is provided as a ceremony for the official closing of the Lord's Day on Sunday evening. Begin with a song and perhaps a time of praise. The following bracketed prayer, adapted from the blessing of Zechariah from Luke 1, may be included at this point, or the Leader may decide to move directly to the next prayer.

LEADER: [Blessed be the Lord God of Israel, for he has visited and redeemed his people, and has raised up a horn of salvation for us in the house of his servant David, as he spoke by the mouth of his holy prophets from of old, that we should be saved from our enemies, and from the hand of all who hate us; to perform the mercy promised to our fathers, and to remember his holy covenant. The oath which he swore to our father Abraham, to grant us that we, being delivered from the hand of our enemies, might serve him without fear, in holiness and righteousness before him all the days of our life. For the day has dawned upon us from on high to give light to those who sit in darkness and in the shadow of death, to guide our feet into the way of peace.]

The Leader pours a cup of wine, raises the cup, and continues as follows.

LEADER: Behold, God is my salvation.

GROUP: *I will trust and will not be afraid.*

LEADER: For God the Lord is my strength and song.

GROUP: *And he has become my salvation.*

LEADER: Therefore with joy you will draw water from the wells of salvation. Salvation belongs to the Lord.

GROUP: *Your blessings be upon your people.*

LEADER: The Lord of hosts is with us.

GROUP: *The God of Jacob is our refuge.*

LEADER: God's people had light and joy and gladness and honor.

GROUP: *So be it with us.*

LEADER: I will lift the cup of salvation and call upon the name of the Lord. Blessed are you, Lord our God, King of the universe, who have created the fruit of the vine.

GROUP: *Amen.*

As the cup is being passed, the following blessing is recited over some bread if the ceremony is being conducted within the context of a meal.

LEADER: Blessed are you, Lord our God, King of the universe, who bring forth bread from the earth.

GROUP: *Amen.*

Distribute the bread and begin the meal.

PRAYER AFTER THE MEAL
(THE CONCLUDING OF THE DAY)

The Leader lifts a cup of wine and recites the following blessing.

LEADER: Blessed are you, Lord our God, King of the universe, who sanctify us through faith in the resurrection of Christ and bless us in this day set apart to celebrate his victory. Blessed are you, Lord our God, who have given us new life in your Son.

GROUP: *Amen.*

Pass the common cup of wine and recite the following prayer while the cup is being passed.

LEADER: Father in heaven, grant that we may begin the working days which draw near to us in peace; freed from all sin and transgression, filled with the joy of your Holy Spirit, and following in the ways of your Son Jesus. May we be fully clothed in him, the New Man, created after your likeness in true righteousness and holiness.

Father of mercy, bless and prosper the work of our hands. Make us fruitful in every good work, unweary in well-doing, knowing that in Christ our labor is not in vain. May all that we do, in word or deed, be to the praise of your glory through Jesus your Son.

Our God and King, guide and defend the people called by your name. Strengthen and prosper all who cherish thoughts of good toward your people, and fulfill their purposes, but frustrate those who devise evil plans against your people, and make their designs of no effect; as it is said, "Take counsel together, but it will come to nothing; speak a word, but it will not stand, for God is with us" (Is 8:10).

Open to us, Father of mercies and Lord of forgiveness, in this week and in the weeks to come, the gates of light and blessing, of redemption and salvation, of heavenly help and rejoicing, of holiness and peace, of the study of your teaching and of prayer. In us also let the Scripture be fulfilled: How beautiful on the mountains are the feet of him who brings good news, who heralds peace, brings happiness, proclaims salvation, who says to Zion, "Your God reigns" (Is 52:7).

GROUP: *Amen.*

The Leader extinguishes the Lord's Day candle, if it has been left burning throughout the day. A song may be sung to conclude.

Part III

Weekday Prayers for Special Seasons

ONE

Advent Prayers

The following prayers, along with the verses of the hymn "O Come, O Come, Immanuel," are based on seven prayers from the early church used in the seven days before Christmas. These prayers address Christ using many of the Messianic titles found in the Old Testament.

An Advent wreath that includes four candles (one for each week) can be used in connection with these prayers which are most appropriately prayed at dinnertime throughout the season.

WEEK ONE OF ADVENT

LEADER: O Immanuel, our King and lawgiver, the expected one of the nations and their Savior, come to save us, O Lord our God.

GROUP: *Come, Lord, come to save us.*

LEADER: O Lord of hosts and leader of the house of Israel, who appeared to Moses in the fire of the burning bush and gave him the Law of Sinai, come to redeem us by your outstretched arm.

GROUP: *Come, Lord, come to save us.*

LEADER: The Spirit of the Lord moved over the darkness of earth and there was light and life. May the burning of this candle remind us of the Lord's coming.

GROUP: *Amen.*

Light the candle.

LEADER: All-powerful God, fill us with the fruits of righteousness that Christ may receive an eager welcome for us at his coming and call us to his side in the kingdom of heaven, where he lives and reigns with you and the Holy Spirit, one God, for ever and ever.

GROUP: *Amen.*

O Come, O Come, Immanuel

    Em   Bm   Am Em
1. O come, O come, Immanuel,
    Bm   C   AmBm Em
  And ransom captive I s -ra- el,
      Am   G D
  That mourns in lonely exile here
     Em   Bm Am Bm G
  Until the Son of God appear.

     G D Em Bm   Am Em
Refrain: Rejoice! R e-joice! Immanuel
     Bm   C   AmEm D Em
  Shall come to thee, O Is -ra- el.

    Em   Bm   Am   Em
2. O come, O come, Thou Lo rd of Might,
     Bm C   Am Bm Em
  Who to thy tribes on S i-n ai's h eight,
    Am   G   D
  In ancient times didst give the Law,
     Em   Bm Am Bm   G
  In cloud, and m a-j esty, and awe.

WEEK TWO OF ADVENT

LEADER: O Root of Jesse, who stands as a banner for the peoples, before whom kings close their mouths, to whom the nations pray, come to deliver us, wait no more.

GROUP: *Come, Lord, come to save us.*

LEADER: O Key of David, and scepter of the house of Israel, who opens and no man shuts, who shuts and no man opens, come and lead the captives from prison and set free those who sit in darkness and the shadow of death.

GROUP: *Come, Lord, come to save us.*

LEADER: The Spirit of the Lord moved over the darkness of earth and there was light and life. May the burning of these candles remind us of the Lord's coming.

GROUP: *Amen.*

Light the two candles.

LEADER: God of power and mercy, open our hearts in welcome. Remove the things that hinder us from receiving Christ with joy, so that we may share his wisdom and become one with him when he comes in glory. We ask this through Christ our Lord, who lives and reigns with you and the Holy Spirit, one God, forever and ever.

GROUP: *Amen.*

O Come, O Come, Immanuel

        Em   Bm   Am   Em
3. O come, Thou Rod of Jesse, free,

      Bm   C   Am Bm Em
Thine own from Satan's   tyr-anny;

     Am   G   D
From depths of hell thy people save,

     Em   Bm   Am Bm   G
And give them vict'ry o'er the grave.

       G D   Em Bm   Am Em
Refrain: Rejoice! Re-joice! Immanuel

        Bm   C   AmEm D Em
Shall come to thee, O Is-ra- el.

        Em   Bm   Am   Em
4. O come, Thou Key of David, come;

      Bm   C   AmBm   Em
And open wide our hea-v'nly home;

     Am   G   D
Make safe the way that leads on high,

     Em   Bm   Am Bm G
And close the path to mi-sery.

WEEK THREE OF ADVENT
(When there are four weeks in Advent)

LEADER: O Morning Star, splendor of eternal light and Sun of Righteousness, come and enlighten those who sit in darkness and the shadow of death.

GROUP: *Come, Lord, come to save us.*

LEADER: O Wisdom that proceeds from the mouth of the Most High, reaching from end to end, mightily disposing of all things, come to teach us the way of knowledge.

GROUP: *Come, Lord, come to save us.*

LEADER: The Spirit of the Lord moved over the darkness of earth and there was light and life. May the burning of these candles remind us of the Lord's coming.

GROUP: *Amen.*

Light the three candles.

LEADER: Lord God, may we your people, who look forward to the coming of Christ, experience the joy of salvation and celebrate his coming with love and thanksgiving. We ask this through our Lord Jesus Christ, who lives and reigns with you and the Holy Spirit, one God, for ever and ever.

GROUP: *Amen.*

O Come, O Come, Immanuel

```
        Em              Bm          Am          Em
5.   O come, Thou Dayspring, come and cheer
        Bm      C     Am Bm     Em
     Our spirits by thine  ad -vent here;
        Am              G          D
     Disperse the gloomy clouds of night,
        Em             Bm        Am Bm    G
     And death's dark shadows,  put to flight.
```

```
         G D       Em Bm         Am  Em
Refrain:  Rejoice! Re-joice! Immanuel
             Bm        C      Am Em D Em
          Shall come to thee, O  Is -ra- el.
```

```
        Em             Bm        Am          Em
6.   O come, Thou Wisdom from on high,
        Bm      C          Am Bm Em
     And order all things far and nigh
        Am              G          D
     To  us the path of knowledge show,
        Em      Bm     Am Bm     G
     And cause us in her  ways to go.
```

WEEK THREE OF ADVENT
(When there are only three weeks of Advent)

LEADER: O Morning Star, splendor of eternal light and Sun of Righteousness, come and enlighten those who sit in darkness and the shadow of death.

GROUP: *Come, Lord, come to save us.*

LEADER: O Wisdom that proceeds from the mouth of the Most High, reaching from end to end, mightily disposing of all things, come to teach us the way of knowledge.

GROUP: *Come, Lord, come to save us.*

LEADER: O King of the nations and their desired one, and cornerstone of the house of God, come and save man whom you formed out of dust.

GROUP: *Come, Lord, come to save us.*

LEADER: The Spirit of the Lord moved over the darkness of earth and there was light and life. May the burning of these candles remind us of the Lord's coming.

GROUP: *Amen.*

Light the three candles.

LEADER: Lord God, may we your people, who look forward to the coming of Christ, experience the joy of salvation and celebrate his coming with love and thanksgiving. We ask this through our Lord Jesus Christ, who lives and reigns with you and the Holy Spirit, one God, for ever and ever.

GROUP: *Amen.*

O Come, O Come, Immanuel

Em   Bm   Am   Em
5.   O come, Thou Dayspring, come and cheer
     Bm   C   AmBm   Em
Our spirits by thine   ad -vent here;
    Am   G   D
Disperse the gloomy clouds of night,
    Em   Bm   Am Bm   G
And death's dark shadows, put to flight.

G D   Em Bm   Am Em
Refrain: Rejoice! Re-joice! Immanuel
     Bm   C   AmEm D Em
Shall come to thee, O   Is -ra- el.

Em   Bm   Am   Em
6.   O come, Thou Wisdom from on high,
     Bm   C   Am Bm Em
And order all things far and nigh
    Am   G   D
To us the path of knowledge show,
    Em   Bm   AmBm   G
And cause us in her ways to go.

Refrain

Em   Bm   Am   Em
7.   O come, Desire of Nations, bind
     Bm   C   AmBm   Em
All peoples in one heart and mind;
    Am   G   D
Bid envy, strife, and quarrels cease;
    Em   Bm   Am Bm   G
Fill the whole world with hea-ven's peace.

WEEK FOUR OF ADVENT

LEADER: O King of the nations and their desired one, and cornerstone of the house of God, come and save man whom you formed out of dust.

GROUP: *Come, Lord, come to save us.*

LEADER: O Immanuel, our King and lawgiver, the expected one of the nations and their Savior, come to save us, O Lord our God.

GROUP: *Come, Lord, come to save us.*

LEADER: The Spirit of the Lord moved over the darkness of earth and there was light and life. May the burning of these candles remind us of the Lord's coming.

GROUP: *Amen.*

Light the four candles.

LEADER: Lord God, fill our hearts with your Holy Spirit, and as you revealed your Son through his coming as man, so lead us through his suffering and death to the glory of his resurrection. We ask this through our Lord Jesus Christ, who lives and reigns with you in the Holy Spirit, one God, for ever and ever.

GROUP: *Amen.*

O Come, O Come, Immanuel

7. O come, Desire of Nations, bind
   All peoples in one heart and mind;
   Bid envy, strife, and quarrels cease;
   Fill the whole world with hea-ven's peace.

Refrain:

    G D   Em Bm   Am Em
Rejoice! Re-joice! Immanuel

        Bm   C   AmEm D Em
Shall come to thee, O   Is -ra- el.

      Em   Bm   Am Em
1. O come, O come, Immanuel,

        Bm   C   Am Bm Em
And ransom captive   Is- ra- el,

      Am   G   D
That mourns in lonely exile here

      Em   Bm   Am Bm   G
Until the Son of God appear.

TWO

Christmas Week Prayers

This prayer is modeled on the Advent prayers, and involves the lighting of one candle (hopefully a large and attractive one!). It is especially appropriate before dinner during Christmas week.

LEADER: Be glorified, eternal Word, Alpha and Omega, Beginning and End, image of God, Light and Life of men.

GROUP: *Glory to you, O Lord.*

LEADER: Be glorified, Son of Man, faithful witness, obedient servant, spotless Lamb, eternal High Priest.

GROUP: *Glory to you, O Lord.*

LEADER: The Lord Jesus Christ said, "I am the Light of the World." May the burning of this candle remind us of his coming in the flesh and our new birth in the Spirit.

GROUP: *Amen.*

Light the candle.

LEADER: Father of Mercy, fill us with your Spirit as we celebrate the incarnation of your Son, that we may rejoice with thanksgiving in your gracious gift and share more fully in his divine life. We ask this through our Lord Jesus Christ, who lives and reigns with you in the Holy Spirit, one God, for ever and ever.

GROUP: *Amen.*

THREE

Good Friday Prayer

This prayer can be used at family prayers before dinner on Good Friday.

LEADER: Father of mercy, as you planted the tree of life
in the Garden of Eden, so you have planted the
cross of your Son in the new paradise, to cancel
the debt of Adam's sin and to open the way to
eternal life.

GROUP: *Glory to you, O Lord.*

LEADER: As you judged the earth by water and saved
Noah by means of the ark, so you judged the
world in the water of your Son's pierced side,
and saved a remnant through the wood of his
cross.

GROUP: *Glory to you, O Lord.*

LEADER: As Abraham's only son, the son he loved, bore
to Moriah the wood of his sacrifice, so your only
beloved Son bore his cross to Golgotha that the
nations might inherit the blessing of Abraham.

GROUP: *Glory to you, O Lord.*

LEADER: As Joseph was sold by his brothers and
reckoned as dead, and then was raised in glory
to the king's right hand, so your Son was

delivered to death by his brothers and raised in
glory to reign at your side.

GROUP: *Glory to you, O Lord.*

LEADER: As the blood of the lamb turned away the angel
of death and delivered Israel from Pharaoh's
rule, so the blood of your Son has saved us from
death and delivered us from bondage to Satan's
dominion.

GROUP: *Glory to you, O Lord.*

LEADER: As the high priest entered the Holy of Holies
with blood to atone for the sins of the people, so
your Son entered the true holy place and
presented the blood that atones for the sins of
the world.

GROUP: *Glory to you, O Lord.*

LEADER: As Moses raised the serpent in the wilderness to
heal those who suffered for their sin, so the Son
of Man was lifted up on the cross to bear our sin
and make us whole.

GROUP: *Glory to you, O Lord.*

LEADER: As Jonah lay three days in the belly of the
whale, and was raised from death to preach
repentance to the Gentiles, so your Son was
raised from the bowels of the earth to turn all
nations to the way of righteousness.

GROUP: *Glory to you, O Lord.*

FOUR

Easter Week Prayers

These prayers are for use at table before breakfast and dinner during the week of celebration following Easter Sunday. They may be used apart from the ordinary daily family prayers, or as an introduction or conclusion to family prayers. If your family would like to light an Easter candle daily at dinner, it would be possible to use these prayers as an introduction to the lighting of the candle.

BREAKFAST

LEADER: Let us arise today and offer praise to the Master, and we shall see Christ, the Sun of Righteousness, who causes life to dawn for all.

GROUP: *Amen! Alleluia!*

LEADER: Christ has risen indeed and has opened for us the gates of salvation. May he pour upon us the abundance of his grace that we may share fully in his resurrection life.

GROUP: *Amen! Alleluia!*

DINNER

LEADER: You did descend, O Christ, into the deepest parts of the earth and did shatter the everlasting bars, which held fast those who were fettered; and on the third day, like Jonah from the whale, you rose from the tomb.

GROUP: *Amen! Alleluia!*

LEADER: Christ has risen indeed and has opened for us the gates of salvation. May he pour upon us the abundance of his grace that we may share fully in his resurrection life.

GROUP: *Amen! Alleluia!*

Part IV

Family Ceremonies for the Christian Feasts

The prayers included in this section are intended to help us honor the Lord as families during the special seasons of the Christian year. They are designed to accompany a festive meal and are built on the model of the Lord's Day ceremony.

These prayers are offered to you as a helpful tool in celebrating the Christian seasons as a family. If they do not work well in your family, you need not feel obligated to use them.

Throughout this section "Leader" is the head of the household, most commonly the father of the family. "Assistant" is either the person next in authority or next in age to the Leader, most commonly the mother of the family. "Group" is all the household members and any guests who may be present. When the letters "G," "A," and "L" appear in parentheses, it indicates that the reading may be done responsively as marked, if more group participation is desired.

ONE

Christmas Eve

THE LIGHTING OF THE CANDLE

The Assistant usually presides over the Lighting of the Candle.

ASSISTANT: The people walking in darkness have seen a great light; on those living in the land of the shadow of death a light has dawned.

(G:) *For to us a child is born, to us a son is given, and the government will be on his shoulders.*

(A:) And he will be called: Wonderful Counselor, Mighty God, Everlasting Father, Prince of Peace.

Heavenly Father, in honor of your Son, Light of the world and Author of life, we are about to kindle the light for the feast of the Incarnation. On this day you revealed your glory to lowly shepherds, announcing the birth of the Morning Star whose light dispels all darkness. On this day heaven and earth resounded with the proclamation of the angelic hosts: Glory to God in the Highest! And on earth peace to men on whom his favor rests!

Father of mercy, may our celebration this day be filled with your peace and heavenly blessing.

Cause us to rejoice with the joy of your Holy
Spirit, and to share in the inheritance of the
saints in light. Keep far from us all anxiety,
darkness, and gloom; and grant that peace,
light, and joy ever abide among us.

GROUP: *For in you is the fountain of life; in your light do we*
see light.

Light the candle and recite the following blessing.

ASSISTANT: Blessed are you, Lord our God, who have sent
your Son to be the Light of the nations and the
glory of your people Israel.

Blessed are you, Lord our God, King of the
universe, who give us joy as we kindle the light
for the feast of the Incarnation.

THE BLESSING OF THE MEAL
AND THE SETTING-ASIDE OF THE DAY AND SEASON

The Opening Proclamation

The following blessing is a proclamation to introduce the meal; it is a
homily by John Chrysostom (from the 4th century).

LEADER: The angels sing. The archangels blend their
voices in harmony. The cherubim hymn their
joyful praise. The seraphim exalt his glory. All
join in praise at this holy feast, beholding the
Godhead here on earth, and man in heaven.
He who is above, now for our redemption
dwells here below; and he that was lowly is by
divine mercy raised.

Bethlehem this day resembles heaven: hearing from the stars the singing of angelic voices and enfolding within itself the Sun of Righteousness. And ask not how; for where God wills, the order of nature yields. For he willed, he had the power, he descended, he redeemed; all things move in obedience to God. This day He Who Is, is born; and He Who Is, becomes what he was not. For when he was God, he became man; yet not departing from the Godhead that is his.

Come, then, let us observe the feast. Come, and we shall commemorate the solemn festival. For this day the ancient slavery is ended, the devil confounded, the demons take to flight, the power of death is broken, paradise is unlocked, the curse is taken away, sin is removed from us, error driven out, truth has been brought back, a heavenly way of life has been planted on the earth, angels communicate with men without fear, and men hold speech with angels.

Why is this? Because God is now on earth and man in heaven. On every side all things commingle. He has come on earth, while being whole in heaven; and while being complete in heaven, he is fully on earth. Though he was God, he became man, not denying himself to be God. Though being the impassible Word, he became flesh. He did not become God. He was God. Therefore he became flesh, so that he whom heaven could not contain, a manger would this day receive.

It is possible to insert here a song and/or a time of praise.

The Blessing of the Wine

Pour wine into the cup, raise it, and recite the following prayer.

LEADER: Let us praise God with this symbol of joy and thank him for the great blessings he has bestowed on us in Christ. In him the fullness of God was pleased to dwell, reconciling earth to heaven, and imparting to us the fullness of life. In him the Word became flesh, enabling men and women of flesh to become children of God. Lord our God, you have revealed to us your glory in Jesus your Son and have made us partakers of the divine nature.

GROUP: *Now we live with him through the Holy Spirit, and we look for the day when we will dwell with him in your everlasting kingdom.*

LEADER: Blessed are you, Lord our God, King of the universe, who have created the fruit of the vine.

GROUP: *Amen.*

The Setting-Aside of the Day and the Season

This blessing welcomes the day and the season and consecrates it to the celebration of the Lord's incarnation.

LEADER: Blessed are you, Lord our God, for the gift of your Son and for this day and this season which are a comemoration of his coming as man. We welcome this time with gladness, and consecrate it to the celebration of his incarnation and of the divine life we have received in him. Look graciously upon your servants and show us your glory. Blessed are you, Lord our God, who favor your people in the days and seasons set aside to your honor.

GROUP: *Amen.*

The Leader drinks from the cup and passes it to the others present.

The Blessing of the Bread

The leader takes bread and recites the following blessing.

LEADER: The eyes of all look to you, O Lord, and you give them their food in due season.

GROUP: *You open your hand, you satisfy the desire of every living thing.*

LEADER: Blessed are you, Lord our God, King of the universe, who bring forth bread from the earth.

GROUP: *Amen.*

Distribute the bread and begin the meal.

BLESSINGS AFTER THE MEAL

After the meal another cup of wine is poured, and the following blessings are recited with the cup raised.

LEADER: Let us bless the Lord.

GROUP: *Blessed be the name of the Lord from this time forth and forever.*

LEADER: Let us bless our God, of whose bounty we have partaken.

GROUP: *Blessed be our God, of whose bounty we have partaken and through whose goodness we live.*

LEADER: Blessed are you, Lord our God, King of the universe, who feed the whole world with your goodness, with grace, with steadfast love and mercy. Through your great goodness food has never failed us. May it not fail us for ever and ever, for your great name's sake, since you nourish and sustain all beings, and do good to all, and provide food for all your creatures whom you have created. Blessed are you, Lord our God, King of the universe, who give food to all.

GROUP: *Blessed be his name forever.*

LEADER: Blessed are you, Lord our God, for by your great mercy we have been born anew to a living hope through the resurrection of Jesus Christ from the dead and to an inheritance that is imperishable, undefiled, and unfading. Blessed are you, Lord our God, King of the Universe, for giving us new life in your Son.

GROUP: *Blessed be his name forever.*

LEADER: Have mercy, Lord our God, upon your people who belong to your Son, the dwelling place in your Spirit. At this season in which we celebrate the incarnation of Christ, grant that the Christian people throughout the world may rejoice greatly in your salvation and grow in the unity for which Jesus prayed on the eve of his sacrifice. Grant also that we in (name of church/community to which family belongs) may radiate that joy and be a sign of that unity and a means of its growth. May all your people be renewed in the power of your Spirit so that we might be without spot or blemish and ready for your Son's return. Blessed are you, Lord our God, King of the universe, ruler and builder of your people, and source of our joy.

GROUP: *Blessed be his name forever.*

The leader drinks from the final cup of wine and passes it to the others present. A song may be sung to conclude.

TWO

Christmas Day

THE BLESSING OF THE MEAL AND
THE SETTING-ASIDE OF THE DAY AND THE SEASON

The Opening Proclamation
The following blessing is a proclamation to introduce the meal.

LEADER: Let us bless the Lord.

GROUP: *Blessed be the name of the Lord from this time forth and forever.*

LEADER: Blessed are you, Lord our God, King of the universe, for revealing your glory to us in Jesus Christ.

You are the one whom no eye can see and no mind can fathom. You showed yourself in the burning bush, in thunder, lightning, earthquake, and cloud, in pillar of fire and trumpet blast. You made your ways known to Moses and your acts to the people of Israel. You spoke by the mouth of holy prophets and dwelt among your people in your holy sanctuary.

(G:) *"And the Word became flesh and dwelt among us, full of grace and truth; we have beheld his glory, glory as of the only Son from the Father."*

(L:) Blessed are you, Lord our God, who have made yourself known in Jesus Christ.

GROUP: *Amen.*

LEADER: Jesus, Redeemer of men, you were begotten by the Father before light was created, as his equal in glory. But you emptied yourself, taking the form of a servant, being born in the likeness of men. Our celebration this day bears witness that you, the only-begotten Son of the Father, have come to be man's salvation.

Therefore, brothers and sisters, let us join our voices this day with the hosts of heaven and with all of creation, and make a joyful noise to him who has won for us salvation.

(G:) *"O sing to the Lord a new song, for he has done marvelous things! His right hand and his holy arm have won for us salvation!"*

It is possible to insert here a song and/or a time of praise.

The Blessing of the Wine

Pour wine into the cup, raise it, and recite the following prayer.

LEADER: Let us praise God with this symbol of joy, and thank him for the great blessings he has bestowed on us in Christ. In him the fullness of God was pleased to dwell, reconciling earth to heaven, and imparting to us the fullness of life. In him the Word became flesh, enabling men and women of flesh to become children of God. Lord our God, you have revealed to us your glory in Jesus your Son and have made us partakers of the divine nature.

GROUP: *Now we live with him through the Holy Spirit, and we look for the day when we will dwell with him in your everlasting kingdom.*

LEADER: Blessed are you, Lord our God, King of the universe, who have created the fruit of the vine.

GROUP: *Amen.*

The Setting-Aside of the Day and the Season

This blessing welcomes the day and the season and consecrates it to the celebration of the Lord's incarnation.

LEADER: Blessed are you, Lord our God, for the gift of your Son and for this day and this season which are a commemoration of his coming as man. We welcome this time with gladness, and con- secrate it to the celebration of his incarnation and of the divine life we have received in him. Look graciously upon your servants and show us your glory. Blessed are you, Lord our God, who favor your people in the days and seasons set aside to your honor.

GROUP: *Amen.*

The Leader drinks from the cup and passes it to the others present.

The Blessing of the Bread

The Leader takes bread and recites the following blessing.

LEADER: The eyes of all look to you, O Lord, and you give them their food in due season.

GROUP: *You open your hand, you satisfy the desire of every living thing.*

LEADER: Blessed are you, Lord our God, King of the universe, who bring forth bread from the earth.

GROUP: *Amen.*

Distribute the bread and begin the meal.

BLESSINGS AFTER THE MEAL

After the meal another cup of wine is poured, and the following blessings are recited with the cup raised.

LEADER: Let us bless the Lord.

GROUP: *Blessed be the name of the Lord from this time forth and forever.*

LEADER: Let us bless our God, of whose bounty we have partaken.

GROUP: *Blessed be our God, of whose bounty we have partaken and through whose goodness we live.*

LEADER: Blessed are you, Lord our God, King of the universe, who feed the whole world with your goodness, with grace, with steadfast love and mercy. Through your great goodness food has never failed us. May it not fail us for ever and ever, for your great name's sake, since you nourish and sustain all beings, and do good to all, and provide food for all your creatures whom you have created. Blessed are you, Lord our God, King of the universe, who give food to all.

GROUP: *Blessed be his name forever.*

LEADER: Blessed are you, Lord our God, for by your great mercy we have been born anew to a living hope through the resurrection of Jesus Christ from the dead and to an inheritance that is imperishable, undefiled, and unfading. Blessed are you, Lord our God, King of the universe, for giving us new life in your Son.

GROUP: *Blessed be his name forever.*

LEADER: Have mercy, Lord our God, upon your people who belong to your Son, the dwelling place of your Spirit. At this season in which we celebrate the incarnation of Christ, grant that the Christian people throughout the world may rejoice greatly in your salvation and grow in the unity for which Jesus prayed on the eve of his sacrifice. Grant also that we in (name of church/community to which family belongs) may radiate that joy and be a sign of that unity and a means of its growth. May all your people be renewed in the power of your Spirit so that we might be without spot or blemish and ready for your Son's return. Blessed are you, Lord our God, King of the universe, ruler and builder of your people, and source of our joy.

GROUP: *Blessed be his name forever.*

As the cup is being passed, the Leader recites the following blessing.

LEADER: When he came to us as man the Son of God scattered the darkness of this world and filled this holy day with his glory. May the God of infinite goodness scatter the darkness of sin and brighten your hearts with holiness.

GROUP: *Amen.*

LEADER: God sent his angels to the shepherds to herald the great joy of our Savior's birth. May he fill you with joy and make you heralds of his gospel.

GROUP: *Amen.*

LEADER: When the Word became man earth was joined to heaven. May he give you his peace and good will, and fellowship with all the heavenly host.

GROUP: *Amen.*

LEADER: May Almighty God bless you, the Father and the Son and the Holy Spirit.

GROUP: *Amen.*

LEADER: May the Lord bless you and keep you; may the Lord make his face to shine upon you and be gracious to you; May the Lord lift up his countenance upon you and give you peace (Num 6:24-26).

GROUP: *Amen.*

A song may be sung to conclude.

THREE

Epiphany Saturday

The feast of Epiphany is traditionally celebrated on January 6, the twelfth day of Christmas. The following ceremony has been prepared as a celebration of the feast on the Saturday nearest to the actual feast day. If these prayers are used on a day other than Saturday evening, omit the lighting of the candle.

THE LIGHTING OF THE CANDLE

The Assistant usually presides over the Lighting of the Candle. For a shortened form of the ceremony you may omit the passage from John 1:1-5.

ASSISTANT: In the beginning was the Word and the Word was with God and the Word was God.

(G:) *All things were made through him and without him nothing was made that has been made.*

(A:) In him was life and the life was the light of men.

(G:) *The light shines in the darkness and the darkness has not overcome it (Jn 1:1-5).*

ASSISTANT: Heavenly Father, in honor of your Son, Light of the world and Author of life, we are about to kindle the light for the Lord's Day. On this day you raised your Son Jesus from the dead and began the new creation. May our celebration of his resurrection this day be filled with your peace and heavenly blessing. Be gracious to us and cause your Holy Spirit to dwell more richly among us.

Father of mercy, continue your loving kindness toward us. Make us worthy to walk in the way of your Son, loyal to your teaching and unwavering in love and service. Keep far from us all anxiety, darkness, and gloom; and grant that peace, light, and joy ever abide among us.

GROUP: *For in you is the fountain of life; in your light do we see light.*

Light the candle and recite the following blessing.

ASSISTANT: Blessed are you, Lord our God, who created light on the first day and raised your Son, the Light of the world, to begin the new creation.

Blessed are you, Lord our God, King of the universe, who gives us joy as we kindle the light for the Lord's Day.

GROUP: *Amen.*

For a short form of the ceremony, the following set of exhortations and responses may be omitted.

LEADER: Let us trust in the Lord and in his saving help.

GROUP: *The Lord is my light and my salvation.*

LEADER: Let us receive his life and rejoice in his presence.

GROUP: *He is the true Light that enlightens every man.*

LEADER: Let us keep his commandments and walk in his ways.

GROUP: *His Word is a lamp to my feet and a light for my path.*

LEADER: Let us proclaim his goodness and show forth his glory.

GROUP: *We are the light of the world and the salt of the earth.*

THE BLESSING OF THE MEAL AND
THE SETTING-ASIDE OF THE DAY AND THE SEASON

The Opening Proclamation
The following blessing is a proclamation to introduce the meal.

LEADER: Let us bless the Lord.

GROUP: *Blessed be the name of the Lord from this time forth and forever.*

LEADER: Blessed are you, Lord our God, King of the universe, for manifesting your glory to us in Jesus Christ.

You are the one whom no eye can see and no mind can fathom. You showed yourself in the burning bush, in thunder, lightning, earthquake, and cloud, in pillar of fire and trumpet blast. You made known your ways to Moses and your acts to the people of Israel. You spoke by the mouth of holy prophets and dwelt among your people in your holy sanctuary.

But in these last days you have manifested your glory through your Son, who dwelt at your side before the foundation of the world.

(G:) *"And the Word became flesh and dwelt among us, full of grace and truth; we have beheld his glory, glory as of the only Son from the Father" (Jn 1:14).*

(L:) Blessed are you, Lord our God, who have made yourself known in Jesus Christ.

GROUP: *Amen.*

LEADER: To you be the praise, Almighty God, for you have redeemed the nations by sending your Son to manifest your glory and establish your reign. The wise men of the nations paid him homage with gifts of gold, incense, and myrrh, and bowed humbly before him, the King of Israel and the heir of all creation. Those who worshiped stars learned from a star to worship him, the Sun of Righteousness, and to recognize him as the Morning Star from on high.

Therefore, brothers and sisters, let us also pay homage to him who has drawn us near by the shedding of his blood and made us fellow-citizens with the saints and members of the household of God; and let us offer him a gift of praise, for through him we all have access in one Spirit to the Father.

It is possible to insert here a song and/or a time of praise.

The Blessing of the Wine
Pour wine into the cup, raise it, and recite the following prayer.

LEADER: Let us praise God with this symbol of joy, and thank him for the great blessings he has bestowed on us in Christ. In him the fullness of God was pleased to dwell, reconciling earth to heaven, and imparting to us the fullness of life. In him the Word became flesh, enabling men and women of flesh to become children of God. Lord our God, you have manifested to us your glory in Jesus your Son and have won for us an eternal salvation.

GROUP: *Now we live with him through the Holy Spirit, and we look for the day when we will dwell with him in your everlasting kingdom.*

LEADER: Blessed are you, Lord our God, King of the universe, who have created the fruit of the vine.

GROUP: *Amen.*

The Setting-Aside of the Day and the Season

This blessing welcomes the day and consecrates it to the celebration of the Lord's incarnation.

LEADER: Blessed are you, Lord our God, for the gift of your Son and for this day and this season which are a commemoration of his coming as man. We welcome this day with gladness, and consecrate it to the celebration of his incarnation and of the divine life we have received in him. Look graciously upon your servants and show us your glory. Blessed are you, Lord our God, who favor your people in the days and seasons set aside to your honor.

GROUP: *Amen.*

The Leader drinks from the cup and passes it to the others present.

The Blessing of the Bread

The Leader takes bread and recites the following blessing.

LEADER: The eyes of all look to you, O Lord, and you give them their food in due season.

GROUP: *You open your hand, you satisfy the desire of every living thing.*

LEADER: Blessed are you, Lord our God, King of the
universe, who bring forth bread from the earth.

GROUP: *Amen.*

Distribute the bread and begin the meal.

BLESSINGS AFTER THE MEAL

After the meal another cup of wine is poured, and the following blessings
are recited with the cup raised.

LEADER: Let us bless the Lord.

GROUP: *Blessed be the name of the Lord from this time forth
and forever.*

LEADER: Let us bless our God, of whose bounty we have
partaken.

GROUP: *Blessed be our God, of whose bounty we have partaken
and through whose goodness we live.*

LEADER: Blessed are you, Lord our God, King of the
universe, who feed the whole world with your
goodness, with grace, with steadfast love and
mercy. Through your great goodness food has
never failed us. May it not fail us for ever and
ever, for your great name's sake, since you
nourish and sustain all beings, and do good to
all, and provide food for all your creatures whom
you have created. Blessed are you, Lord our
God, King of the universe, who give food to all.

GROUP: *Blessed be his name forever.*

LEADER: Blessed are you, Lord our God, for by your great
mercy we have been born anew to a living hope
through the resurrection of Jesus Christ from

the dead and to an inheritance that is imperishable, undefiled, and unfading. Blessed are you, Lord our God, King of the universe, for giving us new life in your Son.

GROUP: *Blessed be his name forever.*

LEADER: Have mercy, Lord our God, upon your people who belong to your Son, the dwelling place of your Spirit. At this season in which we celebrate the manifestation of Christ grant that the Christian people throughout the world may rejoice greatly in your salvation and grow in the unity for which Jesus prayed on the eve of his sacrifice. Grant also that we in (name of church/community to which the family belongs) may radiate that joy and be a sign of that unity and a means of its growth. May all your people be renewed in the power of your Spirit so that we might be without spot or blemish and ready for your Son's return. Blessed are you, Lord our God, King of the universe, ruler and builder of your people, and source of our joy.

GROUP: *Blessed be his name for ever.*

As the cup is being passed, the Leader recites the following blessing from Numbers 6:24-26.

LEADER: May the Lord bless you and keep you; may the Lord make his face to shine upon you and be gracious to you; may the Lord lift up his countenance upon you and give you peace.

GROUP: *Amen.*

A song may be sung to conclude.

FOUR

Easter Sunday

This ceremony is intended for use at the main meal on Easter Sunday. The Christian Passover Service is best suited for Saturday evening, the night before Easter. However, if you want to begin your celebration of Easter on Saturday night using the following ceremony that is fine. You should, however, add the Lighting of the Candle from the Christian Passover Service.

THE BLESSING OF THE MEAL AND
THE SETTING-ASIDE OF THE DAY AND THE SEASON

The Opening Proclamation
The following blessing is a proclamation to introduce the meal.

LEADER: Let us bless the Lord.

GROUP: *Blessed be the name of the Lord from this time forth and forever.*

LEADER: Blessed are you, Lord our God, King of the universe, for redeeming us through Jesus Christ.

He is the true Passover Lamb, who at the great feast paid for us the debt of Adam's sin, and by his blood purified a people for himself.

This is the day when you brought our fathers,

the children of Israel, out of bondage in Egypt, and led them through the Red Sea on dry land.

This is the day when Christ broke the bonds of death and hell, and rose victorious from the grave.

Rejoice now, heavenly hosts and choirs of angels, and let your trumpets shout salvation for the victory of our mighty King.

(G:) *Rejoice and sing now, all the earth, bright with a glorious splendor, for darkness has been vanquished by our eternal King.*

(L:) Rejoice and be glad now, household of the saints, and let your holy courts, in radiant light, resound with the praises of our righteous King.

(G:) *Rejoice now, disciples of Christ, who follow the Lamb wherever he goes, for if we have died with him we shall also rise with him, and share his glory when he returns to reign.*

It is possible to insert here a song and/or a time of praise.

The Blessing of the Wine
Pour wine into the cup, raise it, and recite the following prayer.

LEADER: Let us praise God with this symbol of joy, and thank him for the great victory he has won for us in Christ. By his resurrection he has triumphed over sin, conquered death, defeated Satan, and won for us the riches of an eternal inheritance. We who were perishing through sin have been brought to life together with Christ and raised up with him and made to sit in heavenly places with him. Lord our God, you

have given us a new birth through the
resurrection of Christ.

GROUP: *Now we live with him through the Holy Spirit, and we
look for the day when we will dwell with him in your
everlasting kingdom.*

LEADER: Blessed are you, Lord our God, King of the
universe, who have created the fruit of the vine.

GROUP: *Amen.*

The Setting-Aside of the Day and the Season
This blessing welcomes the day and the season and consecrates it to the
celebration of the Lord's resurrection.

LEADER: Blessed are you, Lord our God, for the gift of life
in your Son Jesus and for this day and this
season which are a commemoration of his
victory over death. We welcome this time with
gladness, and consecrate it to the celebration of
his resurrection and of the new creation
founded in him. Look graciously upon your
servants and show us your glory. Blessed are
you, Lord our God, who favor your people in
the days and seasons set aside to your honor.

GROUP: *Amen.*

The Leader drinks from the cup and passes it to the others present.

The Blessing of the Bread
The Leader takes bread and recites the following blessing.

LEADER: The eyes of all look to you, O Lord, and you
give them their food in due season.

GROUP: *You open your hand, you satisfy the desire of every living thing.*

LEADER: Blessed are you, Lord our God, King of the universe, who bring forth bread from the earth.

GROUP: *Amen.*

Distribute the bread and begin the meal.

BLESSINGS AFTER THE MEAL

After the meal another cup of wine is poured, and the following blessings are recited with the cup raised.

LEADER: Let us bless the Lord.

GROUP: *Blessed be the name of the Lord from this time forth and forever.*

LEADER: Let us bless our God, of whose bounty we have partaken.

GROUP: *Blessed be our God, of whose bounty we have partaken and through whose goodness we live.*

LEADER: Blessed are you, Lord our God, King of the universe, who feed the whole world with your goodness, with grace, with steadfast love and mercy. Through your great goodness food has never failed us. May it not fail us for ever and ever, for your great name's sake, since you nourish and sustain all beings, and do good to all, and provide food for all your creatures whom you have created. Blessed are you, Lord our God, King of the universe, who give food to all.

GROUP: *Blessed be his name forever.*

LEADER: Blessed are you, Lord our God, for by your great mercy we have been born anew to a living hope through the resurrection of Jesus Christ from the dead and to an inheritance that is imperishable, undefiled, and unfading. Blessed are you, Lord our God, King of the universe, for giving us new life in your Son.

GROUP: *Blessed be his name forever.*

LEADER: Have mercy, Lord our God, upon your people who belong to your Son, the dwelling place of your Spirit. At this season in which we celebrate the resurrection of Christ, grant that the Christian people throughout the world may rejoice greatly in your salvation and grow in the unity for which Jesus prayed on the eve of his sacrifice. Grant also that we in (name of church/community to which the family belongs) may radiate that joy and be a sign of that unity and a means of its growth. May all your people be renewed in the power of your Spirit so that we might be without spot or blemish and ready for your Son's return. Blessed are you, Lord our God, King of the universe, ruler and builder of your people, and source of our joy.

GROUP: *Blessed be his name forever.*

As the cup is being passed, the Leader recites the following blessing.

LEADER: When he was raised from the dead the Son of God shattered the iron gates of hell and took the spoil of its captives. May the God of peace soon crush Satan under your feet, and make you sharers in his victory.

GROUP: *Amen.*

LEADER: Those who came to grieve at their Master's tomb departed instead in fear and joy. May the God of all comfort give you strength by his Spirit and fill you with resurrection gladness.

GROUP: *Amen.*

LEADER: When the King of glory ascended into heaven the gates were opened and the angels sang his praise. May God open to you the gates of his temple and assign you a place of honor before his throne.

GROUP: *Amen.*

LEADER: May Almighty God bless you, the Father, the Son, and the Holy Spirit.

GROUP: *Amen.*

LEADER: May the Lord bless you and keep you; may the Lord make his face to shine upon you and be gracious to you; may the Lord lift up his countenance upon you and give you peace (Num 6:24-26).

GROUP: *Amen.*

A song may be sung to conclude.

FIVE

Closing Lord's Day of Easter Week

THE LIGHTING OF THE CANDLE

The Assistant usually presides over the Lighting of the Candle. For a shortened form of the ceremony you may omit the passage from John 1:1-5.

ASSISTANT: In the beginning was the Word and the Word was with God and the Word was God.

(G:) *All things were made through him and without him nothing was made that has been made.*

(A:) In him was life and the life was the light of men.

(G:) *The light shines in the darkness and the darkness has not overcome it (Jn 1:1-5).*

ASSISTANT: Heavenly Father, in honor of your Son, Light of the world and Author of life, we are about to kindle the light for the Lord's Day. On this day you raised your Son Jesus from the dead and began the new creation. May our celebration of his resurrection this day be filled with your peace and heavenly blessing. Be gracious to us and cause your Holy Spirit to dwell more richly among us.

Father of mercy, continue your loving kindness toward us. Make us worthy to walk in the way of your Son, loyal to your teaching and unwavering in love and service. Keep far from us all anxiety, darkness, and gloom; and grant that peace, light, and joy ever abide among us.

GROUP: *For in you is the fountain of life; in your light do we see light.*

Light the candle and recite the following blessing.

ASSISTANT: Blessed are you, Lord our God, who created light on the first day and raised your Son, the Light of the world, to begin the new creation.

Blessed are you, Lord our God, King of the universe, who give us joy as we kindle the light for the Lord's Day.

GROUP: *Amen.*

For a short form of the ceremony, the following set of exhortations and responses may be omitted.

LEADER: Let us trust in the Lord and his saving help.

GROUP: *The Lord is my light and my salvation.*

LEADER: Let us receive his life and rejoice in his presence.

GROUP: *He is the true Light that enlightens every man.*

LEADER: Let us keep his commandments and walk in his ways.

GROUP: *His Word is a lamp to my feet and a light for my path.*

LEADER: Let us proclaim his goodness and show forth his glory.

GROUP: *We are the light of the world and the salt of the earth.*

THE BLESSING OF THE MEAL AND
THE SETTING-ASIDE OF THE DAY AND THE SEASON

The Opening Proclamation
The following blessing is a proclamation to introduce the meal.

LEADER: Brothers and sisters, Christ our Lord is risen. Let us rejoice in his salvation, and declare his mighty deeds.

By his cross he annulled the curse of the tree. By his grave he slayed the might of death. By his rising he paved the way of life, and brought knowledge and salvation to mankind.

Therefore, let us welcome God among us and give him glory.

(G:) *Let us love one another in Christ.*

(L:) May the Holy Spirit be with us as we proclaim the power of Christ's resurrection and exult jubilantly in his praise.

It is possible to insert here a song and/or a time of praise.

The Blessing of the Wine
Pour wine into the cup, raise it, and recite the following prayer.

LEADER: Let us praise God with this symbol of joy, and thank him for the great victory he has won for us in Christ. By his resurrection he has triumphed over sin, conquered death, defeated Satan, and won for us the riches of an eternal inheritance. We who were perishing through sin have been brought to life together with Christ and raised up with him and made to sit in heavenly places with him. Lord our God, you have given us a new birth through the resurrection of Christ.

GROUP: *Now we live with him through the Holy Spirit, and we look for the day when we will dwell with him in your everlasting kingdom.*

LEADER: Blessed are you, Lord our God, King of the universe, who have created the fruit of the vine.

GROUP: *Amen.*

The Setting-Aside of the Day and the Season

This blessing welcomes the day and consecrates it to the celebration of the Lord's resurrection.

LEADER: Blessed are you, Lord our God, for the gift of life in your Son Jesus and for this day and this season which are a commemoration of his victory over death. We welcome this day with gladness, and consecrate it to the celebration of his resurrection and of the new creation founded in him. Look graciously upon your servants and show us your glory. Blessed are you, Lord our God, who favor your people in the days and seasons set aside to your honor.

GROUP: *Amen.*

The leader drinks from the cup and passes it to the others present.

The Blessing of the Bread

The Leader takes bread and recites the following blessing.

LEADER: The eyes of all look to you, O Lord, and you give them their food in due season.

GROUP: *You open your hand, you satisfy the desire of every living thing.*

LEADER: Blessed are you, Lord our God, King of the universe, who bring forth bread from the earth.

GROUP: *Amen.*

Distribute the bread and begin the meal.

BLESSINGS AFTER THE MEAL

After the meal another cup of wine is poured, and the following blessings
are recited with the cup raised.

LEADER: Let us bless the Lord.

GROUP: *Blessed be the name of the Lord from this time forth
and forever.*

LEADER: Let us bless our God, of whose bounty we have
partaken.

GROUP: *Blessed be our God, of whose bounty we have partaken
and through whose goodness we live.*

LEADER: Blessed are you, Lord our God, who feed the
whole world with your goodness, with grace,
with steadfast love and mercy. Through your
great goodness food has never failed us. May it
not fail us for ever and ever, for your great
name's sake, since you nourish and sustain all
beings, and do good to all, and provide food for
all your creatures whom you have created.
Blessed are you, Lord our God, King of the
universe, who give food to all.

GROUP: *Blessed be his name forever.*

LEADER: Blessed are you, Lord our God, for by your great
mercy we have been born anew to a living hope
through the resurrection of Jesus Christ from
the dead and to an inheritance that is
imperishable, undefiled, and unfading. Blessed
are you, Lord our God, King of the universe, for
giving us new life in your Son.

GROUP: *Blessed be his name forever.*

LEADER: Have mercy, Lord our God, upon your people who belong to your Son, the dwelling place of your Spirit. At this season in which we celebrate the resurrection of Christ, grant that the Christian people throughout the world may rejoice greatly in your salvation and grow in the unity for which Jesus prayed on the eve of his sacrifice. Grant also that we in (name of church/community to which family belongs) may radiate that joy and be a sign of that unity and a means of its growth. May all your people be renewed in the power of your Spirit so that we might be without spot or blemish and ready for your Son's return. Blessed are you, Lord our God, King of the universe, ruler and builder of your people, and source of our joy.

GROUP: *Blessed be his name forever.*

As the cup is being passed, the Leader recites the following blessing from Numbers 6:24-26.

LEADER: May the Lord bless you and keep you; may the Lord make his face to shine upon you and be gracious to you; may the Lord lift up his countenance upon you and give you peace.

GROUP: *Amen.*

A song may be sung to conclude.

Pentecost

THE LIGHTING OF THE CANDLE

The Assistant usually presides over the Lighting of the Candle. For a shortened form of the ceremony you may omit the passage from John 1:1-5.

ASSISTANT: In the beginning was the Word and the Word was with God and the Word was God.

(G:) *All things were made through him and without him nothing was made that has been made.*

(A:) In him was life and the life was the light of men.

(G:) *The light shines in the darkness and the darkness has not overcome it (Jn 1:1-5).*

ASSISTANT: Heavenly Father, in honor of your Son, Light of the world and Author of life, we are about to kindle the light for the Lord's Day. On this day you raised your Son Jesus from the dead and began the new creation. May our celebration of his resurrection this day be filled with your peace and heavenly blessing. Be gracious to us and cause your Holy Spirit to dwell more richly among us.

Father of mercy, continue your loving kindness toward us. Make us worthy to walk in the way of your Son, loyal to your teaching and unwavering in love and service. Keep far from us all anxiety, darkness, and gloom; and grant that peace, light, and joy ever abide among us.

GROUP: *For in you is the fountain of life; in your light do we see light.*

Light the candle and recite the following blessing.

ASSISTANT: Blessed are you, Lord our God, who created light on the first day and raised your Son, the Light of the world, to begin the new creation.

Blessed are you, Lord our God, King of the universe, who gives us joy as we kindle the light for the Lord's Day.

GROUP: *Amen.*

For a short form of the ceremony, the following set of exhortations and responses may be omitted.

LEADER: Let us trust in the Lord and in his saving help.

GROUP: *The Lord is my light and my salvation.*

LEADER: Let us receive his life and rejoice in his presence.

GROUP: *He is the true Light that enlightens every man.*

LEADER: Let us keep his commandments and walk in his ways.

GROUP: *His Word is a lamp to my feet and a light for my path.*

LEADER: Let us proclaim his goodness and show forth his glory.

GROUP: *We are the light of the world and the salt of the earth.*

THE BLESSING OF THE MEAL AND THE SETTING-ASIDE OF THE DAY AND THE SEASON

The Opening Proclamation

The following blessing is a proclamation to introduce the meal.

LEADER: Let us bless the Lord.

GROUP: *Blessed be the name of the Lord from this time forth and forever.*

LEADER: Blessed are you, Lord our God, King of the universe, for giving us life by your Holy Spirit.

(G:) *As Moses struck the rock in the desert with his staff and brought forth water to quench Israel's thirst, so Christ your Son has been struck and nailed to a cross so that rivers of living water might flow among all nations.*

(L:) By your great power you have raised your Son Jesus from the dead and seated him in glory at your right hand. You have given him the gift of the promised Holy Spirit, and this Spirit he has poured out upon us from on high.

Blessed are you, Lord our God, for giving us your Spirit through Jesus Christ.

GROUP: *Amen.*

LEADER: Brothers and sisters, great is God's mercy and generous is his gift. By his Spirit we have been born anew, adopted as sons and daughters and given access to his heavenly throne. By his Spirit we have been washed, sanctified, and justified, and his law has been written on our hearts. Even now we have received power from on high, yet it is only a pledge of an eternal inheritance. Therefore, as he has made us one body and a new temple for his praise, let us sing of his glory with one voice and rejoice in the richness of his overflowing goodness.

It is possible to insert here a song and/or a time of praise.

The Blessing of the Wine

Pour wine into the cup, raise it, and recite the following prayer.

LEADER: Let us praise God with this symbol of joy, and thank him for the great blessings he has bestowed on us in Christ. We who were dead through sin and destined for wrath have been raised by the Spirit of Life and presented blameless before God's throne. We who were once slaves and sojourners have now received the Spirit of adoption testifying that we are sons and daughters. Lord our God, you have joined us to yourself in Jesus Christ.

GROUP: *Now we live with him through the Holy Spirit, and we look for the day when we will dwell with him in your everlasting kingdom.*

LEADER: Blessed are you, Lord our God, King of the universe, who have created the fruit of the vine.

GROUP: *Amen.*

The Setting-Aside of the Day and the Season

This blessing welcomes the day and the season and consecrates it to the celebration of the Lord's incarnation.

LEADER: Blessed are you, Lord our God, for the Spirit of Life poured out through your Son Jesus and for this day and this season which are a commemoration of his presence in our midst. We welcome this day with gladness, and consecrate it to the celebration of Christ's victory over death and the new life we have received in the Holy Spirit. Look graciously upon your servants and show us your glory. Blessed are you, Lord our God,

who favor your people in the days and seasons
set aside to your honor.

GROUP: *Amen.*

The Leader drinks from the cup and passes it to the others present.

The Blessing of the Bread
The Leader takes bread and recites the following blessing.

LEADER: The eyes of all look to you, O Lord, and you
give them their food in due season.

GROUP: *You open your hand, you satisfy the desire of every
living thing.*

LEADER: Blessed are you, Lord our God, King of the
universe, who bring forth bread from the earth.

GROUP: *Amen.*

Distribute the bread and begin the meal.

BLESSINGS AFTER THE MEAL

After the meal another cup of wine is poured, and the following blessings
are recited with the cup raised.

LEADER: Let us bless the Lord.

GROUP: *Blessed be the name of the Lord from this time forth
and forever.*

LEADER: Let us bless our God, of whose bounty we have
partaken.

GROUP: *Blessed be our God, of whose bounty we have partaken
and through whose goodness we live.*

LEADER: Blessed are you, Lord our God, who feed the whole world with your goodness, with grace, with steadfast love and mercy. Through your great goodness food has never failed us. May it not fail us for ever and ever, for your great name's sake, since you nourish and sustain all beings, and do good to all, and provide food for all your creatures whom you have created. Blessed are you, Lord our God, King of the universe, who give food to all.

GROUP: *Blessed be his name forever.*

LEADER: Blessed are you, Lord our God, for by your great mercy we have been born anew to a living hope through the resurrection of Jesus Christ from the dead and to an inheritance that is imperishable, undefiled, and unfading. Blessed are you, Lord our God, King of the universe, for giving us new life in your Son.

GROUP: *Blessed be his name forever.*

LEADER: Have mercy, Lord our God, upon your people who belong to your Son, the dwelling place of your Spirit. At this season in which we celebrate the gift of the Spirit, grant that the Christian people throughout the world may rejoice greatly in your salvation and grow in the unity for which Jesus prayed on the eve of his sacrifice. Grant also that we in (name of church/community to which family belongs) may radiate that joy and be a sign of that unity and a means of its growth. May all of your people be renewed in the power of your Spirit so that we might be without spot or blemish and ready for your Son's return. Blessed are you, Lord our God, King of the universe, ruler and builder of your people, and source of our joy.

GROUP: *Blessed be his name forever.*

As the cup is being passed, the Leader recites the following blessing from Numbers 6:24-26.

LEADER: May the Lord bless you and keep you; may the Lord make his face to shine upon you and be gracious to you; may the Lord lift up his countenance upon you and give you peace.

GROUP: *Amen.*

A song may be sung to conclude.

Part V

Christian Passover Service

Many members of the Christian people have found the annual celebration of the Christian Passover Service to be a helpful way to celebrate the death and resurrection of the Lord. It is best observed on Saturday night before Easter or during Easter Week, but it is possible to do anytime during Holy Week.

The meal preparations as well as the ceremony itself are somewhat complicated. It may be best to first participate in this service before organizing and leading it yourself.

ONE

Instructions

IN MANY LANGUAGES the word for Easter is "Passover." This reveals a truth often unrecognized by Christians: Easter is simply the Christian Passover. The Passover feast celebrated annually by the Jewish people is fulfilled in Christ's sacrificial death and victorious resurrection. Our observance of the Passover can thus teach us the true significance of Christ's redeeming sacrifice and provide a fitting way to celebrate the events which have brought us freedom.

THE HISTORICAL ORIGIN AND FULFILLMENT OF PASSOVER

Old Testament Origin. The first Passover occurred in Egypt, while the people of Israel were still in bondage. Exodus 1-15 tells the story of Israel's enslavement in Egypt and her miraculous deliverance at the hand of Moses. In Exodus 11-13 we read of the tenth plague which broke Pharaoh's stubborn resistance and allowed Israel to go free. In this plague the Lord slew all the firstborn males in the land of Egypt, except those whose doorposts were sprinkled with the blood of the Passover lamb; thus, the firstborn of Israel were spared. The Lord passed over the home of the Israelites, but judged the homes of the Egyptians.

Old Testament Commemoration. In Exodus 12-13 the Lord commands the people of Israel to keep the Passover as an annual celebration commemorating the deliverance from Egypt. Each household was to sacrifice a Passover lamb, eat unleavened bread and bitter herbs, and rejoice in God's redemption. We read in 2 Chronicles of the great Passover feasts kept by Hezekiah (30:1-27) and Josiah (35:1-19). The Jewish people have observed the customs of the Passover to this very day.

New Testament Fulfillment. The New Testament teaches us that Christ has fulfilled the Passover (Jn 19:36; Ex 12:46; 1 Cor 5:7-8). His death and resurrection, which occurred at Passover time, redeems us from enslavement to sin, death, Satan, and the world. His blood, like the blood of the first Passover lamb, protects God's people from the angel of death and breaks the oppressive reign of Satan.

New Testament Commemoration. At the Last Supper, which was probably a Passover meal, Jesus instituted a custom by which his disciples were to remember and celebrate his death and resurrection (Lk 22:7-38). This custom, the Lord's Supper, is a New Covenant Passover meal that commemorates the sacrifice of the true Passover Lamb and brings us into special fellowship with God.

Easter, The Annual Christian Passover. The early Christians celebrated Easter as the Christian Passover feast. Since the death and resurrection of Christ occurred during Passover, the annual celebration of the New Covenant redemption was perpetually wedded to the Passover. Just as Christ is the true Passover Lamb, of which the lambs sacrificed in Egypt were but a type and foreshadowing, so the Christian Passover feast is the fulfillment of the annual Old Covenant rite, in which God's deliverance is recalled and celebrated.

Future Fulfillment. The final fulfillment of the Passover is in the messianic kingdom (Lk 22:15-16). The redemption accomplished in Christ's death and resurrection will only be fully manifested when he comes again to judge the wicked (as Egypt was judged) and to bring his chosen ones into their eternal resting place (the true land of promise). Then the disciples of Jesus will eat and drink at table with their Messiah and rejoice together in his victory (Lk 22:28-30).

THE EXODUS EVENTS AS PROPHETIC TYPES

Christian teachers in the New Testament and the early church saw all of the main events of Israel's exodus from Egypt as *types* (models, foreshadowings, prefigurements) of God's redemption in Christ. For example, the apostle Paul identifies the passage through the Red Sea with baptism and the desert gift of manna and water with Communion (1 Cor 10:1-5). This is a very helpful way for Christians to understand the preparatory events of the Old Testament and their fulfillments in the New Testament. The following types should be recalled annually at the Christian Passover Service:

Egypt—a type of "the world," alienated from God and bound up in sin; also, a type of sin itself and a sinful way of life.

Pharaoh and his Army—a type of Satan and his evil legions.

The Blood of the Passover Lamb—a type of the blood of Christ, which wards off the angel of death and purchases redemption.

The Passage through the Red Sea—a type of baptism.

The Pillar of Fire and Cloud—a type of the Holy Spirit, Christ's presence among us.

The Manna from Heaven and the Water Flowing from the Rock—a type of the Lord's supper.

The Giving of the Covenant and the Law at Sinai—a type of the New Covenant in the blood of Christ and the Pentecostal outpouring of the Holy Spirit.

Entry into the Promised Land—a type of our new life in Christ and its consummation in the New Jerusalem.

PRACTICAL SUGGESTIONS FOR OBSERVING THE CHRISTIAN PASSOVER SERVICE

The atmosphere of a Passover service should be joyful and prayerful. There should be many opportunities for songs and spontaneous worship. There should also be times when children and adults can ask questions about the Passover and grow in their understanding.

The Passover service is supposed to be a family affair. Therefore, the children should be encouraged to participate as much as possible. If there are many younger children present (younger than reading age), the Leader could consider deleting some of the optional readings and Gospel passages which are marked off in parentheses. Older children can be included in the service by reading the Scripture passages, performing the part of the youngest son, or reading other portions of the service. The Leader should shape the length and content of his instruction according to the age and attentiveness of his audience. This Passover service is flexible and open to some modification, though the basic structure and message should not be altered.

If the Christian Passover Service is to be a success, the Leader must invest some time in preparation. He should study the order of the service, the relevant Scripture passages, and the present explanation, and he should think through how he will teach on the passage from Deuteronomy 26. He should decide what to delete and what to add, who will read which parts, who will perform the role of the youngest son, what songs should be sung, and how the celebration will flow practically. He should also familiarize himself with the layout of the table and the location of the special ritual platters containing such items as unleavened bread, bitter herbs, and haroseth (see the following glossary of terms for an explanation of this word).

GLOSSARY OF PASSOVER SYMBOLS AND CUSTOMS

In order to convey the richness of the Passover meal, the Leader must understand the various symbols and customs. A brief summary of the most important items follows:

Seder—the word "Seder" means order, referring to the Passover service conducted during the Passover meal.

Blessings—the most common and important form of Jewish prayer is the blessing. Each blessing usually begins, "Blessed are you, Lord our God ...," and proceeds to indicate in some way the object which is being blessed (sometimes it is not an object, but is instead an action). Rather than asking God to bless something, the Jews would thank God for that thing and understand that the thing was thereby specially consecrated.

   a) **Wine and Bread**—especially important are the blessings over the wine and the bread. The initial blessing over wine, called the *Kiddush,* or Sanctification, precedes every Sabbath and festival meal, and proclaims the holiness of the day and consecrates it specially to the Lord. The blessing over the bread is the thanksgiving for the meal, bread as the traditional staple food symbolizing the meal as a whole.

b) **Four Cups of Wine**—four cups of wine are passed around the table and drunk. The four cups represent the four chief expressions of God's deliverance in the Book of Exodus: "I shall bring them forth," "I shall deliver them," "I shall redeem them," and "I shall take them unto me as a nation."

c) **The Common Cup and Loaf**—the common cup and the common loaf express the unity of the people, their brotherhood as sons of Abraham and co-heirs of the promise. It also represents their common share in the blessing over the bread and wine.

Lamb—the lamb represents the lamb which was sacrificed in the temple and eaten by Jewish families in the land of Israel. All its blood was drained out; the commandment of the Lord that none of its bones be broken was carefully observed. It was roasted on a cross-like spit of pomegranate branches, and it reminded the Jews of the lamb whose blood had saved their ancestors at the great Exodus.

Unleavened Bread—it was called the "bread of affliction" because it was made of flour and water alone. It represents the bread baked by the Jews during their hasty flight from Egypt, when there was no time for leavening. The three pieces of unleavened bread on the main plate represent the three classes of Israelites: the Priests, the Levites, and the ordinary Israelites.

Bitter Herbs—these herbs represent the bitter suffering endured by the Israelites while slaves in Egypt.

Haroseth—a mixture of chopped apples, nuts, cinnamon, and wine, with its reddish color recalled the mortar used by the Jews in building the palaces and pyramids of Egypt during their centuries of forced labor.

Green Vegetables—a characteristic relish used at festive meals in ancient Palestine. The greens represent spring, and the salt water in which they are dipped represent the tears shed by the people of Israel while in bondage in Egypt.

Egg—a hard-boiled egg represents the festival offering in the temple during an important festival.

Cup of Elijah—a cup that was filled with wine and left for Elijah, the prophet who was to return as the herald of the Messiah. It was believed that the Messiah would come on a Passover.

SEDER MENU

Ritual Platter:
1 hard-boiled egg	parsley
horseradish	haroseth
lamb bone	

Main Meal—any meat (other than pork) is acceptable for the main dish. Lamb and chicken are two commonly used meats, but beef or fish would also be possibilities. Some lamb is also needed for the ritual platter.

Side Courses—vegetables and dessert are, like the main dish, flexible. The haroseth will be the salad, and unleavened bread will replace normal leavened bread. Enough unleavened bread should be available so that people can eat it during the meal (it tastes good with butter).

Appetizer—each person may have a hard-boiled egg of his or her own to dip in the salt water.

Ceremonial Items:
unleavened bread	haroseth
celery	salt water
horseradish	

Festival Wine—for use in the four blessings, but also as a beverage during the meal.

BASIC HAROSETH RECIPE

3 large, firm apples
1 cup walnut pieces
about 1/3 cup Concord grape wine

1 teaspoon cinnamon
2-3 teaspoons honey

Finely chop the apples and the walnuts, then mix the rest of the ingredients. This recipe makes two and one-fourth cups of haroseth which serves ten to twelve people.

TABLE SETTING

From the beginning of the Seder the following articles should be set on the table:

Green Herb—pieces of lettuce or parsley, enough for one piece per person, perhaps a little more.

Bitter Herb—usually horseradish, used ceremonially as a dip, enough for each person.

Unleavened Bread—enough for at least one piece per person, perhaps more.

Cups of Salt Water—for the green herb, set on the table so as to be accessible to all.

Haroseth—in one or more bowls.

Festival Candle—set near the front of the table, where the Assistant should sit (beside the Leader).

Cup of Elijah—a cup filled with wine and set near the front of the table.

Wine Goblet—to be used as a common cup.

Ceremonial Trays—both of these trays should be set in front of the Leader.

1. **Seder Plate**—a large plate containing a hard-boiled egg, a large lamb bone, some bitter herbs, a piece of parsley, and some haroseth. The contents of this tray are ceremonial only, and will not be consumed during the meal.

2. **Bread of Affliction**—a plate containing three pieces of unleavened bread, each wrapped individually in a napkin, and stacked one on top of the other. Like the seder plate, these pieces of unleavened bread are ceremonial, and will not be consumed during the meal.

TWO

Outline

I. Initial Blessings
- The Lighting of the Candle
- The Setting-Aside of the Feast
    The First Cup of Wine, the "Cup of Sanctification"
    (consecrating the celebration to the Lord)
- The Green Herb

II. Recital of the Story of the Deliverance from Egypt
- Initial Proclamation
- The Four Questions
- The Answer
    Explanation of the Deliverance from Egypt
    Explanation of the Passover Symbols
- A Song of Praise
- The Second Cup of Wine, the "Cup of Salvation"

III. The Festive Meal
- Grace over Unleavened Bread and Bitter Herbs
- The Meal
- Blessings after the Meal
    The Third Cup of Wine, the "Cup of Blessing"

IV. Conclusion
- Final Praises
- Blessing the Fourth Cup of Wine, the "Cup of Praise"

THREE

The Christian Passover Service

"Leader" is the head of the household, most commonly the father of the family. "Assistant" is either the person next in authority or next in age to the Leader, most commonly the mother of the family. "Group" is all the household members and any guests who may be present.

INITIAL BLESSINGS

THE LIGHTING OF THE CANDLE

The Assistant usually presides over the Lighting of the Candle. After an opening song, the Assistant recites the following prayers.

ASSISTANT: Christ, our Passover Lamb, has been sacrificed. Therefore, let us celebrate the feast not with the old leaven of malice and evil, but with the unleavened bread of sincerity and truth.

Heavenly Father, in honor of your Son, Light of the world and Author of life, we are about to kindle the light for the Passover of Christ. On this day you delivered us from the bondage of sin and made us heirs of your heavenly kingdom. May our victory celebration this day be filled with your peace and heavenly blessing. Be gracious to us and cause your Holy Spirit to dwell more richly among us.

Father of mercy, continue your loving kindness toward us. Make us worthy to walk in the way of your Son, loyal to your teaching and unwavering in love and service. Keep far from us all anxiety, darkness, and gloom; and grant that peace, light, and joy ever abide among us.

GROUP: *For in you is the fountain of life; in your light do we see light.*

Light the candle and recite the following blessings.

ASSISTANT: Blessed are you, Lord our God, who ransomed a people for yourself by the blood of Jesus your Son, and fulfilled the Scripture by raising him from the dead.

Blessed are you, Lord our God, King of the universe, who give us joy as we kindle the light for the Feast of the Passover of Christ.

GROUP: *Amen.*

ASSISTANT: Blessed are you, Lord our God, King of the universe, who have kept us alive and sustained us and brought us to this season. May our home be consecrated, O God, by the light of your face, shining upon us in blessing and bringing us peace.

GROUP: *Amen.*

THE SETTING-ASIDE OF THE FEAST (THE FIRST CUP)

The Leader pours wine into the cup, raises it, and recites the following blessings.

LEADER: Blessed are you, Lord our God, King of the universe, who have created the fruit of the vine.

GROUP: *Amen.*

LEADER: Blessed are you, Lord our God, King of the universe, who chose us in Christ before the foundation of the world, that we should be holy and blameless before you. In your love, O God, you give us seasons for gladness, holidays and times for rejoicing, even this day of the feast of the Passover of Christ, the season of our freedom. We welcome this time with gladness, and consecrate it to the celebration of Christ's victory over sin and death and the salvation provided for us in him. Look graciously upon your servants and show us your glory. Blessed are you, Lord our God, who favor your people in the days set aside to your honor.

GROUP: *Amen.*

The leader drinks from the cup and passes it to the others present.

The words of Luke 22:14-18 probably refer to this first cup of wine, the "Cup of Sanctification." These words can be read while the cup is being passed, or the Leader can pause and then move directly to the next prayer.

LEADER: And when the hour came, he sat at table, and the apostles with him. And he said to them, "I have earnestly desired to eat this passover with you before I suffer; for I tell you I shall not eat it until it is fulfilled in the kingdom of God." And he took a cup, and when he had given thanks he said, "Take this, and divide it among yourselves; for I tell you that from now on I shall not drink of the fruit of the vine until the kingdom of God comes" (Lk 22:14-18).

The Green Herb

All take a piece of parsley or lettuce and dip it in salt water. The Leader then recites the following blessing, after which all eat the herb.

LEADER: Blessed are you, Lord our God, King of the universe, who have created the fruit of the earth.

GROUP: *Amen.*

RECITAL OF THE STORY OF THE DELIVERANCE FROM EGYPT

INITIAL PROCLAMATION

The Leader lifts up the ceremonial plate containing the three pieces of unleavened bread and uncovers the top piece. He reads the following proclamation while holding the plate.

LEADER: This is the bread of affliction which our fathers ate in the land of Egypt. All who are hungry, let them come and eat. All who are needy, let them come and celebrate the Passover with us. May it be God's will to redeem us from all trouble and sin and all servitude. Next year at this season may we and all our brothers and sisters sit at table in the New Jerusalem and enjoy the glorious liberty of the children of God.

The Leader returns the plate, covers the bread, and pours the second cup of wine.

THE FOUR QUESTIONS

The youngest boy present stands and reads the following questions.

YOUNGEST BOY: *Why is this night different from all other nights?*

On all other nights we eat either leavened or unleavened bread. Why on this night do we eat only unleavened bread?

On all other nights, we eat all kinds of herbs. Why on this night do we eat especially bitter herbs?

On all other nights, we do not dip herbs in any condiment. Why on this night do we dip them in salt water and haroseth?

On all other nights, we eat without special festivities. Why on this night do we hold this Passover service?

THE ANSWER

Explanation of the Deliverance from Egypt

LEADER: Once we were slaves of Pharaoh in Egypt, and the Lord our God brought us out from there with a strong hand and an outstretched arm. Now if God had not brought out our fathers from Egypt, then we might still be enslaved to Pharaoh in Egypt. Therefore, even were we all wise, all people of understanding, and even if we were all old and learned in the Law, it would still be our duty to tell the story of the departure from Egypt. And the more one tells of the departure from Egypt, the more he is to be praised.

And for us who know that Christ, the true Passover Lamb, has redeemed us from bondage to sin and death, the saying is also true: The more one tells of the departure from Egypt, the more he is to be praised.

The Leader now reads the following passage from Deuteronomy 26:5-9. He should give a commentary on the passage, first describing the original exodus from Egypt depicted in the Book of Exodus, and then explaining how it is fulfilled in Christ. It is best to read the whole passage first, then to read it verse by verse with a commentary after each verse.

LEADER: My father Jacob was a wandering Syrian who went down to Egypt with a small household and lived there as an alien; and there he became a nation great, strong, and numerous. And the Egyptians maltreated and oppressed us, imposing hard labor upon us. Then we cried to the Lord, the God of our fathers, and he heard our cry and saw our affliction, our toil, and our oppression; and the Lord brought us out of Egypt with a strong hand and an outstretched arm, with terrifying power, with signs and wonders; and he brought us into this country, and gave us this land flowing with milk and honey (Dt 26:5-9).

My father Jacob was a wandering Syrian who went down to Egypt with a small household and lived there as an alien. (For background see Genesis 45-47.)

And there he became a nation great, strong, and numerous. (For background see Exodus 1:7.)

And the Egyptians maltreated and oppressed us, imposing hard labor upon us. (For background see Exodus 1:8-22.)

Then we cried to the Lord, the God of our fathers, and he heard our cry and saw our affliction, our toil, and our oppression. (For background see Exodus 3:1-12.)

And the Lord brought us out of Egypt with a strong hand and an outstretched arm, with terrifying power, with signs and wonders. (For background see Exodus 5-11.)

And he brought us into this country, and gave us this land flowing with milk and honey.

The Leader now recites the following thanksgiving, and after each line the Group responds, "It would have been enough for us."

LEADER: Had he brought us out of Egypt, and not executed judgment against them,

GROUP: *It would have been enough for us.*

LEADER: Had he executed judgment against them, and not divided the sea for us,

It would have been enough for us.

Had he divided the sea for us, and not drowned our oppressors in it,

It would have been enough for us.

Had he drowned our oppressors in it, and not helped us forty years in the desert,

It would have been enough for us.

Had he helped us forty years in the desert, and not fed us manna,

It would have been enough for us.

Had he fed us manna, and not brought us to Mount Sinai,

It would have been enough for us.

Had he brought us to Mount Sinai, and not given us the Law,

It would have been enough for us.

Had he given us the Law,
and not brought us into the Promised Land,

It would have been enough for us.

Had he brought us into the Promised Land,
and not given us the temple,

It would have been enough for us.

Had he given us the temple,
and not sent us his Son, the Messiah,

It would have been enough for us.

Had he sent us his Son, and
not given him up to die for our sins on the cross,

It would have been enough for us.

Had he given up his Son to die on the cross,
and not raised him from the dead in victory,

It would have been enough for us.

Had he raised him from the dead,
and not sent us his Holy Spirit,

It would have been enough for us.

LEADER: How much more do we have to be thankful for the boundless blessings of the all-merciful God: that he brought us out from Egypt, executed judgment against them, divided the sea for us, drowned our oppressors in it, helped us forty years in the desert, fed us with manna, brought us to Mount Sinai, gave us the Law, brought us into the Promised Land, gave us the temple, sent us his Son, gave him up to die for our sins on the cross, raised him from the dead in victory, and sent us his Holy Spirit.

The following passage is taken from a second century Easter sermon by
Melito of Sardis. For a shorter form of the service, this passage may be
omitted.

LEADER: Jesus Christ is the Passover of our salvation. He
was led away as a lamb and sacrificed as a
sheep. He delivered us from servitude to the
world as from the land of Egypt. He released us
from bondage to the devil as from the hand of
Pharaoh and sealed our souls by his own Spirit
and our bodies by his own blood.

This is the one who covered death with shame
and who plunged the devil into mourning as
Moses did Pharaoh. This is the one who smote
lawlessness and deprived injustice of its
offspring, as Moses deprived Egypt. This is the
one who delivered us from slavery into
freedom, from darkness into light, from death
into life, from tyranny into an eternal kingdom,
and who made us a new priesthood and a
special people forever. This one is the Passover
of our Salvation.

EXPLANATION OF THE PASSOVER SYMBOLS

LEADER: Rabbi Gamaliel used to say: "Whoever does not
explain the following three symbols at the
Passover Seder has not fulfilled his duty—the
Passover lamb, the unleavened bread, and the
bitter herbs."

YOUNGEST
BOY: *The Passover lamb which our fathers ate in temple
days, what was the reason for it?*

LEADER: It was because the Holy One, Blessed be he,
passed over the houses of our ancestors in

Egypt, as it is written, "And you shall say it is the Passover offering for the Lord who passed over the houses of the children of Israel in Egypt when he struck Egypt and spared our houses. And the people bowed their heads and worshiped" (Ex 12:26-27).

And the true Passover Lamb is Jesus Christ, who gave his life as a sacrifice upon the cross, as it is written, "Behold, the Lamb of God, who takes away the sin of the world" (Jn 1:29), and "Christ, our Passover Lamb, has been sacrificed" (1 Cor 5:7).

YOUNGEST BOY: *This unleavened bread which we eat, what is the reason for it?*

LEADER: It is because there was not time for the dough of our ancestors in Egypt to become leavened before the King of kings, the Holy One, blessed be he, revealed himself to them and redeemed them, as it is written, "And the dough which they had brought out from Egypt they baked into cakes of unleavened bread, for it had not leavened, because they were thrust out of Egypt and allowed no time even to get food ready for themselves" (Ex 12:39).

And the true unleavened bread is the purity and holiness of a life lived in Christ, as it is written, "Let us celebrate the feast not with the old leaven of malice and evil, but with the unleavened bread of sincerity and truth" (1 Cor 5:8).

YOUNGEST BOY: *These bitter herbs which we eat, what is their meaning?*

LEADER: It is because the Egyptians embittered the lives of our forefathers in Egypt, as it is written, "And

they embittered their lives with hard labor:
with mortar and bricks, with every kind of
work in the fields; all the work which they
made them do was rigorous" (Ex 1:13-14).

And the true bitter herb is the grief and sorrow
of sin that Christ tasted on our behalf, as it is
written, "Surely he has borne our griefs and
carried our sorrows; yet we esteemed him
stricken, smitten by God, and afflicted. But he
was wounded for our transgressions, he was
bruised for our iniquities; upon him was the
chastisement that made us whole, and with his
stripes we are healed" (Is 53:4-5).

In every generation, one must look upon
himself as if he personally had come out of
Egypt, as it is written, "And you shall tell your
son on that day, 'It is because of what the Lord
did for me when I went forth from Egypt,'" (Ex
13:8). For it was not our fathers alone that the
Holy One, blessed be he, redeemed; he also redeemed us with them, as it is said, "He brought
us out from there that he might give us the land
which he pledged to our fathers" (Dt 6:23).

A SONG OF PRAISE

LEADER: Therefore it is our duty to thank and to praise
in song and prayer him who performed all these
wonders for our fathers and for us. He brought
us out from slavery to freedom, from anguish to
joy, from sorrow to festivity, from darkness to
great light. Let us therefore sing before him a
new song. Praise the Lord!

It is possible to insert here a song and/or a time of praise.

THE SECOND CUP OF WINE

The Leader raises the cup and recites the following blessing.

LEADER: Blessed are you, Lord our God, who redeemed
us and our fathers from Egypt, and brought us
to this day to eat unleavened bread and bitter
herbs. May we rejoice in your salvation and
always say, "The Lord be praised."

Blessed are you, Lord our God, King of the
universe, who have created the fruit of the vine.

GROUP: *Amen.*

The Leader drinks from the cup and passes it around the table.

THE FESTIVE MEAL

GRACE OVER UNLEAVENED BREAD
AND BITTER HERBS

The Leader takes a piece of unleavened bread and blesses it with the
following words.

LEADER: The eyes of all look to you, O Lord, and you
give them their food in due season.

GROUP: *You open your hand, you satisfy the desire of every
living thing.*

LEADER: Blessed are you, Lord our God, King of the
universe, who bring forth bread from the earth.

GROUP: *Amen.*

LEADER: Blessed are you, Lord our God, King of the
universe, who gave the commandment
concerning the eating of unleavened bread.

GROUP: *Amen.*

The Leader breaks the bread into small pieces and distributes a piece to each person.

The words of Matthew 26:26 probably refer to this point in the ceremony. These words can be read while the unleavened bread is broken and distributed, or the Leader can pause and then move directly to the next prayer.

LEADER: Now as they were eating, Jesus took bread, and blessed, and broke it, and gave it to the disciples and said, "Take, eat; this is my body" (Mt 26:26).

Each person places some of the bitter herbs and some haroseth between two pieces of unleavened bread.

LEADER: Let us combine the unleavened bread and the bitter herbs, as it is written: "With unleavened bread and with bitter herbs, they shall eat it."

Blessed are you, Lord our God, King of the universe, who gave the commandment concerning the eating of bitter herbs.

GROUP: *Amen.*

All now eat the unleavened bread with bitter herbs and haroseth.

THE MEAL

The festive meal is eaten at this point.

THE BLESSINGS AFTER THE MEAL

It is possible to insert here a song. The third cup of wine should be poured.

LEADER: Let us bless the Lord.

GROUP: *Blessed be the name of the Lord from this time forth and forever.*

LEADER: Let us bless our God, of whose bounty we have partaken.

GROUP: *Blessed be our God, of whose bounty we have partaken and through whose goodness we live.*

LEADER: Blessed are you, Lord our God, who feed the whole world with your goodness, with grace, with steadfast love and mercy. Through your great goodness food has never failed us. May it not fail us for ever and ever, for your great name's sake, since you nourish and sustain all beings, and do good to all, and provide food for all your creatures whom you have created. Blessed are you, Lord our God, King of the universe, who give food to all.

GROUP: *Blessed be his name forever.*

LEADER: Blessed are you, Lord our God, for by your great mercy we have been born anew to a living hope through the resurrection of Jesus Christ from the dead and to an inheritance that is imperishable, undefiled, and unfading. Blessed are you, Lord our God, King of the universe, for giving us new life in your Son.

GROUP: *Blessed be his name forever.*

LEADER: Have mercy, Lord our God, upon your people who belong to your Son, the dwelling place of your Spirit. At this season in which we celebrate the Passover of Christ, grant that the Christian people throughout the world may rejoice greatly in your salvation and grow in the unity for which Jesus prayed on the eve of his sacrifice. Grant also that we in (name of church or community to which family belongs) may radiate that joy and be a sign of that unity and a means of its growth. May all your people be renewed in the power of your Spirit so that we might be without spot or blemish and ready for your Son's return. Blessed are you, Lord our God, King of the universe, ruler and builder of your people, and source of our joy.

GROUP: *Blessed be his name forever.*

The Leader raises the cup and recites the following blessing.

LEADER: Blessed are you, Lord our God, King of the universe, who have created the fruit of the vine.

GROUP: *Amen.*

The Leader drinks from the cup, passes it around the table, then fills it again.

The words of Matthew 26:27-29 probably refer to this point of the ceremony. These words can be read while the cup is being passed, or the Leader can pause and move directly to the concluding prayers.

LEADER: And he took a cup, and when he had given thanks he gave it to them, saying, "Drink of it, all of you; for this is my blood of the covenant, which is poured out for many for the forgiveness of sins. I tell you I shall not drink again of this fruit of the vine until that day when I drink it new with you in my Father's kingdom" (Mt 26:27-29).

CONCLUSION

For a shorter form of the service, the following reading in brackets may be omitted.

LEADER: [The soul of all living things shall bless your name, O Lord our God; the spirit of all flesh shall ever adore and extol your fame, our King.

Were our mouths filled with singing as the sea
and our tongues uplifted in song as the waves
and our lips with praises as the heavens, and
our eyes shining as the sun and the moon, and
our hands stretched out as the eagles of the
skies, and our feet swift as the hinds, we would
still not be able to offer proper thanks to you, O
Lord our God and God of our Fathers, and to
praise your name one thousandth share or even
a tenth of one thousandth share for the great
goodness you bestowed upon our fathers and
upon us.

From Egypt you redeemed us, O Lord our God,
and from the house of bondage you liberated
us. In famine you fed us, in plenty you
sustained us, from the sword you saved us,
from pestilence you delivered us, from severe
sickness you spared us.

Therefore the limbs you have fashioned within
and the spirit of life which you have breathed
into us, and the tongue which you have placed
in our mouth, they shall all thank, praise, extol,
glorify, exalt, adore, hallow and give sovereignty
to your name; for every mouth shall give thanks
to you, and every tongue shall pledge fealty to
you; and every knee shall bend to you, and
every living thing shall bow down to you; all
hearts shall revere you, and all souls shall sing
to your name.]

You are God by the power of your might, great
by the glory of your name, almighty forever and
inspiring awe by your deeds. You are the King
enthroned sublimely and exalted. By the mouth
of the upright you shall be praised, and by the

words of the righteous you shall be lauded; by the tongue of the faithful you shall be exalted, and in the midst of the holy you shall be hallowed.

Blessed are you, O Lord, King extolled in praises.

GROUP: *Amen.*

The Leader lifts the cup and recites the following blessing.

LEADER: Blessed are you, Lord our God, King of the universe, who have created the fruit of the vine.

GROUP: *Amen.*

The Leader drinks from the cup and passes it around the table.

LEADER: The Passover service is ended. As we were worthy to celebrate it this year, so may we perform it in future years. O Pure One in heaven above, bring us to the heavenly Jerusalem in joy. Maranatha, come Lord Jesus!

A song may be sung to conclude.